CAMBRIDGE LIBRARY COLLECTION

Books of enduring scholarly value

Perspectives from the Royal Asiatic Society

A long-standing European fascination with Asia, from the Middle East to China and Japan, came more sharply into focus during the early modern period, as voyages of exploration gave rise to commercial enterprises such as the East India companies, and their attendant colonial activities. This series is a collaborative venture between the Cambridge Library Collection and the Royal Asiatic Society of Great Britain and Ireland, founded in 1823. The series reissues works from the Royal Asiatic Society's extensive library of rare books and sponsored publications that shed light on eighteenth- and nineteenth-century European responses to the cultures of the Middle East and Asia. The selection covers Asian languages, literature, religions, philosophy, historiography, law, mathematics and science, as studied and translated by Europeans and presented for Western readers.

A Grammar of the High Dialect of the Tamil Language, Termed Shen-Tamil

Published in 1822, but completed in manuscript form almost 100 years earlier, this work was designed to accompany Beschi's earlier *Grammar of Common Tamil*. While the latter enabled the student to speak the language, this reissue offers a way into reading Tamil's classical literature with its complexity of thought and technique. One of the earliest and most distinguished pioneers in the field of Tamil studies, C.G. Beschi (1680–1747) was a Jesuit missionary in Madura, as well as a translator and composer of Tamil poetry. Since this treatise was not previously formally printed, this translation by B.G. Babington (1794–1866), from the original Latin, is based on a collation of texts, transcriptions and copies. In his preface, Babington outlines errata and problems stemming from this process, and makes explanatory notes where necessary. The work nevertheless remains a groundbreaking study of an ancient and complex language by a sensitive and thorough scholar and a gifted translator.

Cambridge University Press has long been a pioneer in the reissuing of out-of-print titles from its own backlist, producing digital reprints of books that are still sought after by scholars and students but could not be reprinted economically using traditional technology. The Cambridge Library Collection extends this activity to a wider range of books which are still of importance to researchers and professionals, either for the source material they contain, or as landmarks in the history of their academic discipline.

Drawing from the world-renowned collections in the Cambridge University Library and other partner libraries, and guided by the advice of experts in each subject area, Cambridge University Press is using state-of-the-art scanning machines in its own Printing House to capture the content of each book selected for inclusion. The files are processed to give a consistently clear, crisp image, and the books finished to the high quality standard for which the Press is recognised around the world. The latest print-on-demand technology ensures that the books will remain available indefinitely, and that orders for single or multiple copies can quickly be supplied.

The Cambridge Library Collection brings back to life books of enduring scholarly value (including out-of-copyright works originally issued by other publishers) across a wide range of disciplines in the humanities and social sciences and in science and technology.

A Grammar of the High Dialect of the Tamil Language, Termed Shen-Tamil

To Which is Added,
an Introduction to Tamil Poetry

Costantino Giuseppe Beschi
Translated by B.G. Babington

CAMBRIDGE
UNIVERSITY PRESS

CAMBRIDGE UNIVERSITY PRESS

Cambridge, New York, Melbourne, Madrid, Cape Town,
Singapore, São Paolo, Delhi, Mexico City

Published in the United States of America by Cambridge University Press, New York

www.cambridge.org
Information on this title: www.cambridge.org/9781108055116

© in this compilation Cambridge University Press 2013

This edition first published 1822
This digitally printed version 2013

ISBN 978-1-108-05511-6 Paperback

A

GRAMMAR.

OF

THE HIGH DIALECT

OF THE

TAMIL LANGUAGE,

TERMED

SHEN-TAMIL:

TO WHICH IS ADDED,

AN INTRODUCTION

TO

TAMIL POETRY.

BY THE REVEREND FATHER C. J. BESCHI,

Jesuit Missionary in the Kingdom of Madura.

TRANSLATED FROM THE ORIGINAL LATIN,

BY

BENJAMIN GUY BABINGTON,

Of the Madras Civil Service.

𝔐𝔞𝔡𝔯𝔞𝔰:

PRINTED AT THE COLLEGE PRESS: 1822.

TRANSLATOR'S PREFACE.

No one can be considered thoroughly versed in the Tamil language, who is not skilled in both the dialects into which it is distinguished. A knowledge of the common Tamil is, indeed, sufficient for the conduct of all ordinary business, in our intercourse with the Natives; but to those who aspire to read their works of science, or to explore their systems of morality, an acquaintance with the Shen Tamil, or polished dialect, in which all their valuable books are written, and all their learning is contained, is quite indispensable. It is not, by any means, pretended, that the studies of all who learn the language should be extended to this dialect. The requisite proficiency could not be attained, but at the expence of much time and labour, which might in general be directed to more useful acquirements. But that there should be some who may be capable of examining the qualifications of those who teach, as well as of those who learn the language, and of ascertaining the merits of native works of science, appears to be requisite, inasmuch as the improvement of the people should be an object of solicitude.

A grammar of the high Tamil, therefore, as affording the means of attaining this capability, appeared to be a desideratum; and it was a conviction of its utility in promoting knowledge, as we find from his preface, which made the original author undertake this work.

Beschi seems to have had a more perfect acquaintance with Tamil literature, than any foreigner who ever undertook the study; perhaps, than any native of modern times. His voluminous works, both in prose and poetry, composed in Tamil, as well as his translations from it, are held in great esteem ; and it is a singular fact, that one of the best original grammars of that language now extant, is the production of his pen.

His grammar of the low Tamil is already in general use, and is an invaluable introduction to that dialect: the present work contains all that a student needs to know respecting the high Tamil. The two together complete the subject, and no branch of Tamil philology is now inaccessible.

It may, perhaps, be thought by some, that this work should have been more detailed, and that it should have been at least as copious as the author's grammar for the Natives; but we must bear in mind, that two of the five heads into which Tamil grammar is distinguished, are here omitted, for reasons stated in the author's preface. In comparing this work with Tonnúl-Vilaccam, it must also be remembered, that, as the latter, in order to assist the memory of the Natives, who always learn their sciences by rote, is written in poetry, the conciseness of the diction must be frequently sacrificed on that account. That treatise is likewise loaded with examples, and each Sútram is succeeded by a long commentary in prose. When all these causes of difference are duly weighed, I believe it will be found, that Tonnúl-Vilaccam contains very little, if any, useful information, which is not comprised in the present work.

Nearly a century has elapsed since this treatise was written, and as it has never been printed, the copies now extant have, by frequent transcription, become very erroneous, and even obscure. This was the case with the copy from which this version was made; and it was only by the collation of several texts, that the faulty passages have been amended or explained. The text, as it now stands, is consistent with itself; and therefore bears internal evidence that it does not any where materially differ from the true reading.

The present translation was undertaken with a view to facilitate the student's labours. The style of the original is by no means elegant, and not unfrequently difficult; and although, among the students of the College, for whose use particularly these sheets are intended, many are, no doubt, sufficiently acquainted with Latin to read it, yet few could do so without some labour; and as the subject is in itself rather dry and abstruse, it appeared desirable to remove as far as possible, all extrinsic difficulties.

The Translator is aware that there are some who will differ from him on this point, and will argue, that no one who could read the original, would trust to a translation. This opinion is certainly not borne out by experience. The English version of Beschi's low Tamil grammar, which is the work of a foreigner, and so badly executed as to be, in some parts, scarcely intelligible, is nevertheless used by the students of the College; and although the original may there be had, while the translation must be purchased at a considerable price, not one in ten has ever read the former, whilst every one is in possession of the latter.

In the translation, the object has been throughout, carefully to preserve the sense of the author, without a scrupulous adherence to his turn of expression. This, indeed, was the less necessary; because, the work being one of science, not of fancy, to explain the meaning was, of course, the principal end in view. It is, however, believed, that no material deviations will be met with.

Beschi, in his preface, tells us, that he has not quoted authorities for his examples, because the names of the authors even of the most celebrated works are now unknown. This reason, so far as the name of the author is concerned, is certainly satisfactory; but it by no means accounts for his omission to refer to the works themselves. The Translator, who was obliged to search them, in order to correct the examples, thought it would add authority to these to subjoin the reference to each. This has been done whenever it could be found : there are, however, some quotations which still remain unsupported; but these have been employed immemorially in the Native grammars, and, it is probable, were originally taken from authors of repute, whose writings have long since perished.

The original works which have been consulted on these occasions, need not be described. None could be procured, remarkable either for accuracy or genuineness; so that it was necessary to consider the quotation as correct, when it was consistent in its sense, and an example of the rule which it was meant to illustrate.

Tamil scholars differ in their mode of distinguishing, in writing, mute consonants from those which are joined with the inherent short vowel, and the letter சு from the medial long ā ா; the mode adopted here has been, to place a dot over all mute consonants, and to mark the letter சு by an inflection of its right foot.

The Tamil stanzas quoted in this work have been divided into lines, which no one will doubt to be a much clearer way of writing poetry than the native method, according to which, little distinction is made between verse and prose; the number only of each stanza being interposed. From the commencement of the second part of the grammar, the lines too have been separated into feet, which will enable the student readily to perceive the construction of a stanza, and will assist in rendering this subject, in itself somewhat intricate, intelligible and easy.

A few notes have been added, for the purpose of pointing out what appeared to be inaccuracies, and which, if allowed to pass without notice, might mislead the learner. At the same time, it is with great deference that the Translator has ventured to dissent, on these occasions, from the learned author. The number of these annotations might have been considerably increased, had the object been to collect all the information which could be obtained, and to discuss the contradictory opinions of grammarians and their commentators. But this, it is evident, would have been at variance with the author's plan, of which brevity and consistency appear to have been the leading principles. A more copious treatise is not necessary to those who have resolved to attain a critical knowledge of high Tamil; because, by the time they have become masters of these rudiments and their application, they will have acquired, from practice, whatever was too easy and obvious for insertion here; and if further information is desired, they will be able to search for it in native grammars : while, for those who read merely to satisfy curiosity, or to obtain a general notion of high Tamil, even this short work contains more than is required.

The AUTHOR'S INTRODUCTION.

C. J. BESCHI.

TO THE PIOUS MISSIONARIES OF THE SOCIETY OF JESUITS.

GREETING.

When I last year presented you with a grammar of the common dialect of the Tamil language, with the view of aiding your labours as ministers of the gospel, I promised that I would shortly say something respecting the superior dialect; but my time being occupied by more important duties, the work was deferred longer than I had at first expected. Urged, however, by the pressing solicitations of my friends, no longer to delay making public the information which I had amassed by a long and ardent study of the abstruse works of ancient writers, but to communicate the fruit of my labours, I resolved to avail myself of the little leisure which I could spare from more weighty avocations, and freely to impart what it had cost me no inconsiderable pains to acquire. I was further encouraged to the task, by my sense of the very favorable reception which my introduction to the common dialect had universally met with. Let me intreat the same indulgence for the present work. That the study will be one of considerable difficulty, I do not pretend to deny; but the labour will not want its reward. Among the Natives themselves, very few can now be found who are masters of the higher dialect. He among them who is acquainted even with its rudiments, is regarded with respect; but should he quote their abstruse works, he is listened to with fixed admiration; what praise, then, would they not bestow on a foreigner, whom they should find deeply versed in a science which they themselves consider scarcely attainable?

They will readily attend to the teaching of one whose learning is the object of their admiration. And as this may evidently lead to the honor of religion, and promote the salvation of those about us, I am satisfied that this consideration alone, operating on zeal like yours, will suffice to excite you to the study of this dialect, notwithstanding the difficulties that attend it.

But since almost all the Tamil works in this dialect are in verse, I trust you will not deem it improper, if I venture to draw your attention to heathen poets, and to the study of poetry. In former times, ST. JEROME was severely censured for having, by the introduction of examples from the poets, sullied the purity of the church with the pollutions of the heathen. ST. JEROME, in his learned reply, demonstrates, that the apostle PAUL repeatedly cites from the poets, in his epistles, and that the most exemplary among the fathers not only made frequent use of illustrations from the writings of laymen, but that, even by their own poetry, they, far from polluting, embellished the church. These remarks apply with particular force in this country, the natives of which are swayed not so much by reason as by authority; and what have we from their own authors to adduce in aid of truth, except the verses of their poets? For, since all their writings are in verse, they have reduced to metre their rules of art, and even the rudiments of their language: whence, they naturally suppose, that he who does not understand their poetry, is totally ignorant. Moreover, there are excellent works in Tamil poetry on the subject of the divine attributes and the nature of virtue; and if, by producing texts from them, we turn their own weapons against themselves, they will blush not to conform to the precepts of teachers in whom they cannot glory without condemning themselves. If we duly consider what has been said, we shall be satisfied, that, in this country especially, it is highly proper in a minister of the gospel to read the poets, and to apply himself to the study of poetry.

The first person who wrote a grammatical treatise on this dialect, and who is therefore considered as its founder, is supposed to have been a devotee named Agattiyan, respecting whom many absurd stories are related. From the circumstance of his dwelling in a mountain called

Podiamalei, in the South of the Peninsula, the Tamil language has obtained the name of தென்மொழி, or *Southern*, just as the Grandonic is termed வடமொழி, or *Northern*, from the supposition that it came from the Northward. A few of the rules laid down by Agattiyan have been preserved by different authors, but his works are no longer in existence. After his time, the following persons, with many others, composed treatises on this dialect, viz. Palacàyanàr, Ageiyanàr, Nattattanàr, Mayēsurer, Cattiyanàr, Avinayanàr, Càkkeippàdiniyàr. The works of all these writers have perished, and we know that they existed only by the frequent mention of their names in books which are now extant. One ancient work, written by a person called Tolcàppiyanàr, (*ancient author*) is still to be met with ; but, from its conciseness, it is so obscure and unintelligible, that a devotee named Pavananti was induced to write on the same subject. His work is denominated Nannùl, a term that corresponds exactly to the French *belles lettres*, and the Latin *Litteræ humaniores*. Although every one is familiar with this title, few have trod even on the threshold of the treatise itself. The author divides his subject into five parts, which are comprised in the following line :

எழுத்துச்சொற்பொருளியாப்பணி.

1st. எழுத்து, Ezjuttu. *Letters.* This head treats on pronunciation and orthography.

2d. சொல், Chol. *Words ;* which-are composed of letters. This head treats of the noun, the verb, and the other parts of speech.

3d. பொருள், Poruí. *Matter ;* or the mode in which, by uniting words, a discourse is formed. This head treats on amplification, the affections of the mind, &c. It is subdivided into Agapporuí, and Purapporuí ; that is to say, into *matter interior* and *exterior.* The former relates to the passions and affections of the mind, which act on man internally ; the latter, to things external to man.

4th. யாப்பு, Yàppu. *Versification.* The Tamil writers confine their remarks on this head to the subject of prosody, and say nothing of the art of poetry.

5th. அணி, Aṇí. *Embellishment.* This head treats on tropes and figures. The term Panjavilaccanam, which we here used, is the general expression for these five heads.

Pavananti not having completed his design, his Nannùl comprises only the two first heads, viz. *Letters* and *Words;* on each of which he has treated at considerable length. On his death, a person named Nàrccavirà-ja Nambi, took up the subject, and wrote on the third head, or *matter.* A devotee called Amirdasàgaren, (sea of nectar,) composed a treatise on the fourth head, or *Versification,* which he entitled Càrigei ; and lastly, a person named Tandi wrote on the fifth head, or *Embellishment :* his work was called from him Tandiyalancàram ; the word Alancàram being the same as Aṇí.

On *Amplification* and *Embellishment,* the third and fifth heads, I shall say nothing ; because my readers are already acquainted with the rhetoric of Europe, to which nothing new is added by the Tamil authors. As I have also treated fully on the *Letters* in the grammar of the common Tamil, the remarks which I shall here offer on that subject will be confined to the peculiarities which exist in the superior dialect. This work will, accordingly, be divided into two parts ; the first of which will relate to *Letters* and *Words;* the second, to *Versification.* Under the latter head, I shall take occasion to say something respecting the art of Tamil poetry.

In the course of this work, much will be purposely omitted, either as being not of frequent use, or attainable by a little practice : my object being, merely to explain the first rudiments of the language, and thereby to remove the more prominent obstacles which oppose its attainment.

I shall frequently adduce examples from the most esteemed authors ; with the view, as well of illustrating the rules which I may lay down, as of initiating the student into the practice of the language. As many of these examples will appear without the name of the author being annexed, it becomes necessary to explain, that the Tamil writers do not usually prefix them to their compositions ; and although the names of some have been handed down to us by their commentators, yet the number of commentaries which have been written on poetical works, is small; and even in these, the author's name is not always mentioned. For instance, the commentator on the poem Chintàmani speaks in terms of praise of its author, whom he styles the master of all the learned. He may indeed with justice be called the prince of Tamil poets, but of his name the commentator does not inform us. Nor are we to suppose that the work itself is called after its writer; Chintàmani being only an appellation bestowed on the hero of the poem, whose name is Sívagan. In like manner, we learn that the poet so well known under the name of Tiruvalluven, who has left us a work containing 1,330 distichs, was of the low tribe of Paraya, but of his real name we are ignorant: for although he had no less than seven commentators, not one of them has mentioned it. Valluvan, is the appellation by which soothsayers, and learned men of the Paraya tribe are distinguished; and Tiru here signifies *divine*, in the sense in which we say *the divine Plato*. Such is the origin of this honorary title, which has now come to be used as the real designation of the person to whom it is applied. Again, we have a collection of moral sentences worthy of Seneca himself, written by a woman who, if we may believe tradition, was sister to the last mentioned author; but her real name also is unknown, although she is always called Auviyàr, a title which is appropriated to aged matrons. There is another work which I shall occasionally quote, and the title of which is Nàladiyàr, which contains 400 epigrams on moral subjects. The origin of this name is said to be as follows: eight thousand poets visited the court of a certain prince, who, being a lover of the muses, treated them with kindness, and received them into favor: this excited the envy of the bards who already enjoyed the royal patronage, and in a short time they succeeded so completely in their attempt to prejudice their master against the new comers, that the latter found it necessary to consult their safety by flight; and, without taking leave of their host, decamped in the dead of night. Previous to their departure, each poet wrote a venbà on a scroll, which he deposited under his pillow. When this was made known, the king, who still listened to the counsels of the envious poets, ordered the scrolls to be collected, and thrown into a river, when 400 of them were observed to ascend, for the space of four feet, nàladi, against the stream. The king, moved by this miraculous occurrence, directed that these scrolls should be preserved; and they were accordingly formed into a work, which, from the foregoing circumstance, received the name of Nàladiyàr.

I have now said all that I think necessary by way of introduction to this work. In conclusion, I have only to assure the student, that if he will apply himself to the perusal of the ancient authors, he will find their writings to be by no means undeserving of his attention. Farewell!

Ides of September 1730.

CONTENTS.

PART THE FIRST.

CONTENTS.

PART the SECOND.

Of Tamil Poetry.

Of Asei.

Of Sír.

Of Talei.

Of Adi.

Of Todei.

iv

CONTENTS.

CONTENTS.

PART THE FIRST.

CHAP. I.

SECTION THE FIRST.

OF LETTERS.

I. To the rules respecting letters which are given in my other grammar, and which are equally applicable here, the following are added.

In naming the letters in this dialect, those which are short are distinguished by the affix கரம், and those which are long, by காரம்; thus, அ is termed அகரம், and ஆ, ஆகாரம்; த, தகரம் and தா, தாகாரம். Hence, Tiruval l'uven says, அகரமுதலவெழுத்தெல்லாம், &c. *The alphabet begins with* அ. In the Shen Tamil or higher dialect the Grant ham characters are never used; but to the letters employed in the common dialect, one consonant is added, which is termed ஆய்தம், and is written thus ஃ: this letter resembles the consonant *g*, obscurely uttered, with a deep guttural sound: it has the force of a consonant, but is never joined with a vowel; the effect, therefore, of inserting it in any word, is to render the syllable which precedes it long by position, although by nature it be short. Thus, if அது be written அஃது, the first syllable becomes long in presody, from its position before two consonants. Example.

அன்பின்வழிய துயிர்நிலை யஃதில்லார்க்
கென்புதோல்போர்த்தவுடம்பு

திருவ-௮, அதி-௰, குற.

Here if, instead of அஃதில்லார, the poet had written அதில்லார், the first syllable of the word would have been short, which would not have suited the metre. In order to explain the poet's meaning, the Student must be apprized that, in Tamil, the body is occasionally termed உயிர் நிலை, *the seat of life*. The distich may be rendered: *That is the seat of life which walketh in the paths of affection: the bodies of such as lack affection are only bones covered with skin.*

II. The letters are distinguished by the Tamil grammarians into various classes.

First. The whole alphabet is divided into vowels—consonants—and consonants joined to vowels, that is, syllables. The vowels are twelve in number, and are termed உயிர் ; the consonants, exclusive of ஆய்தம், are eighteen in number, and are termed மெய், or ஒற்று; and consonants joined to vowels, are termed உயிர்மெய், *animated bodies.*

Secondly. The vowels are distinguished into five short, குறில் ; அ, இ, உ, எ, ஒ, and seven long, நெடில்; ஆ, ஈ, ஊ, ஏ, ஐ, ஓ, ஔ. This distinction has been fully explained in the grammar of the common dialect.

Thirdly. The consonants are divided into three classes: 1st வல்லினம், *hard letters,* or, as the Greeks term them, *rough :* they are, க, ச, ட, த, ப, ற. 2nd மெல்லினம், *soft letters :* they are, ங, ஞ, ண, ந, ம, ன. 3rd இடையினம், *mediate letters,* that is, neither hard nor soft: they are, ய், ர, ல, வ, ழ, ள. This division must be carefully remembered, as it will throw much light on what is to follow.

Fourthly. The consonants are distinguished into மொழிமுதலெழுத்து *initial* and மொழிஇறுதிஎழுத்து *final;* that is, such as may begin, and such as may end a word. The initials are nine; viz. க. ச. த. ப. ஞ. ந. ம. ய. வ.: the finals are eight; * viz. ண. ம. ன. ய. ர. ல. ழ. ள.: we may,

---

* This enumeration of the finals is supported by the following rule from an original grammar intitled Virasózhiyam வீரசோழியம்.

எ று மகர ண கர க கடா முயிடை யினத்தி

ெவ்வு றுபவகா மொழித்தைதக டுள்ளாக தெழி இயிருமெ

ஈ்துமதிெமைஙகட ஐருமங்கஇெட மெவிற றெற னறு

கூறு நத:ழி இருக ற றமுத்தாெ மெனபார்கே லவவிீர்ேயெ.

சக இயபபடலம் - எ, பாடடஇ

ம & the two ன's (ன & ண): *of the mediate letters 5, rejecting வ: and of the beauteous vowels twice five are declared to be final letters in Tamil, whose region is between the virtue-bestowing Véngadam (Tripaty) and Cumari (Cape Comarin)—Oh thou ornamented with handsome bracelets !*

It is here asserted, that this class consists of ண, ம, ன all the mediate letters except வ, and ten of the vowels. But in Tonnúl vil'accam, (எழுத். வ், நூத.) Beschi has followed எழ்றூவ், (எ முத். இஉ, நூத்.) where வ also is stated to be a final. He has omitted it here, probably because of it's unfrequent occurrence. In Tolcappiyam தொல்காபபியம், we read வகாகிெவ்விகான மொழிற் றற த, மொழிமராியல் சஇ, நூ. *Four words terminate in the letter வ they are* இவ் *these* அவ் *those* (distant) உவ் *those* (between இவ் *and* அவ்) தெவ் *enmity.*

however, meet with one or two instances in this dialect, where the imperative of a verb ends in ரு. as உகிரு *imp:* of உகிருசல் *to suck,* ‡ I am aware that in the common dialect, we have words which begin with ர, as ரண்டு *two,* சோரமம் *hair;* and with ல, as லாபம் *gain,* சோலகம் *metal:* but in Nannu'l we are told, that இ or உ † must be prefixed to such words; and that we ought to write இரண்டு, உசோரமம், இல்லபம், உசோலகம். The author adds that, even to words beginning with ய, it is not only allowable, but elegant to prefix இ, so that for யாளை *elephant* we may write இயாளை, and for யாத்திரை *journey,* இயாத்திரை. In this dialect, words commencing with ட, as டாபபு *a list,* and with ற, as றேறு நகைச *filthiness,* are never used.

Fifthly. Of the twelve vowels, the following three, உ, இ and ஓ, have two states; in one of which they are integral, in the other abbreviated. I shall notice each of these vowels separately.

உ. If this vowel be joined to a hard letter, and be preceded by a syllable long by nature, as in நாடு *country,* ஆறு *river,* காடு *wood;* or long by position, as in கற்பு *chastity,* அச்சு *a stamp;* or if it be preceded by two short syllables, as in அரிது *difficult,* கழுகு *a vulture:* in all these cases, it is termed குற்றியலுகரம், *abbreviated* உ. Hence, while to the utterance of a short vowel one measure of time, called மாத்திரை, is allotted, to this abbreviated உ only half that length is allowed; and this is the cause, why it is always cut off before another vowel. On the other hand, although in the word கடு, for instance, உ is joined to ட, which is a hard letter, yet, since it is preceded by one syllable only, and that a short one, and is not followed by a double consonant, it is neither abbreviated, nor can it be cut off; as has been explained in the grammar of the common Tamil, No. 13. In this case, it is called குற்றுகரம், *integral* உ.

இ. We have said, that to words beginning with ய, as யாளை, யாமம் *midnight,* it is reckoned elegant to prefix இ, and to write இயாளை, இயா

---

‡ and also in ந; as பொருந, imp of பொருந்தல் *to join* v. n.

† In Nannu'l we are told, that to some words beginning with ர, அ also is prefixed, as, அரங்கம் *an isle.*

மம. This vowel is then termed குற நியகிளாம, and the measure allotted to it is half a மாததிளா. In verse, if the metre require it, it may be considered as a consonant, and not as a syllable: Thus,

குழவிகி இயாழி கிடு தனபர்தமமககண
மழவிசஉசா றடேகளாதவர்

இருவ - ஏ, அதி - சீர, குற.

Here, இயாழ has been used for யாழ ; but if the இ were considered as a vowel, the measure of the verse would be destroyed. The passage may be rendered : *Those may praise the pipe and the lute, who have never heard the prattle of children of their own :* which is as much as to say, that the voice of these is sweeter to a parent's ear than any music.

ஐ. This vowel, when it occurs in monosyllables, or when it becomes அளெபெடை, (a term which we shall presently explain,) is never abbreviated ; but it is abbreviated in the middle or end of polysyllables, and is then called ஐகாரகுறுகலம. This is no longer pronounced, as in other cases, ai ; but soft, as ei ; and is short in verse.

Sixthly. அளெபெடை is a certain protraction of the sound of any letter. The seven long vowels may be lengthened by அளெபெடை, which in this case, is termed உமெளெபெடை. This is done, by adding to the long letter its corresponding short one, which last must be written in its primitive form. Thus அ is added to ஆ : இ to ஈ, &c. The letter இ is made to correspond with ஐ, and உ with ஒள †. In pronouncing a syllable which is lengthened by அளெபெடை, the sound is to be protracted ; and it is considered, in verse, equivalent to two syllables. Example :

கறறதறுஅாயபயஙெனணெடொல்வாதினிவ
எற்று பெடாாழாதிஜொனின

இருவ - முதல், அதி - உ, குற.

What is the fruit of learning, if they (the learned) *worship not at the goodly feet of Him the purely wise ?* Here, if from the word டொழாஅர், we take away the அ, which has been inserted by அளெபெடை, the verse will be lame.

---

† Because இ *i* is the last component of the diphthong ஐ *ai ;* as உ *u* is of the diphthong ஒள *au.*

III. Of the consonants, the following eleven, க. ஞ: ண. ந. ம. ன. ய. வ. வ: ள. ழ், when they are ஒற்று, that is, not united with vowels, may be doubled, both in writing and pronouncing, by அனடெபடை; which in this case, is termed ஒற்றனடெபடை: Thus, for அங்கணெ *there*, we may write அங்க்கணெ. If the consonant be already double, a third may be added by this figure: Thus, மின்னு *lightning* may become மின்ன்னு; consonants thus doubled are sometimes, though rarely, considered, in verse, as one syllable. ஒற்றனடெபடை is a figure which is allowed only in poetry, and even there it is seldom used: உயிரனடெபடை, on the contrary, occurs repeatedly even in prose; particularly the அனடெபடை of the letter உன, which is employed, both in verse, though the metre may not require it, and in prose, when the conjunction உம is to be added to a word ending in உ: thus, அதூம is put for அதுவும, செயவதூம for செயவதுவும, and சொலவதூம for சொலவதுவும.

> தமமையிகழநததமைதாடெபாறுபயபதன நிமற
> ஒற்மடையிகழநதவிவஃபெபயயததாழ்மடை
> யெரிவாயநிலையததழிழ்ழவர்கொலெனறு
> பரிவதூடெஞசானடெரார்கடன

நால்டியார் · ம்உ ⁿஅடு - அ ₂கவி.

If, in the last line, the poet had written simply பரிவதூம, the metre would still have been good. The sentiment contained in the foregoing passage would not be unworthy even of a Christian: *It is the duty of the wise not only to forgive despite; but also to pity those who are about to fall into hell the place of fire, as the fruit of the despite they have done them.*

IV. I take this opportunity to explain the nature of the மாத்திணெ, by which the Tamils measure the quantity of their letters: a மாத்திணெ is defined to be, that space of time which is occupied by the twinkling of an eye, or the snapping of a finger. Of these spaces, one is allotted to a short syllable, two to a long one, and three to a long syllable to which a short one has been added by அனடெபடை. One space and a half is allowed to the letter ஈ, * when abbreviated; but to உ and இ, when abbreviated, only half a space. Half a space is also allowed to consonants, and to the letter ஆய்தம்; but a consonant doubled by அளபெடை occupies one entire space.

SECTION THE SECOND.

OF ORTHOGRAPHY.

V. The rules for orthography detailed in the grammar of the common dialect, (No. 17 to 32,) must be rigidly observed in this dialect. To those rules I shall here add a few remarks; dwelling particularly on such points as appear to be most important,

First. It is a general rule of Tamil orthography, that soft or mediate letters are never doubled after a long letter. Hence, since in the word ஆயாவும், ய், being a mediate letter, cannot be doubled after ஆ, which is a long letter, we may immediately perceive that it is to be read *áyayávum*. In the word கானடன் since ன is a soft letter, we must read *kánanádan*.

Secondly. Words which are usually written with a reduplicated letter, provided that letter be either soft or mediate, may drop the reduplication, or not, as best suits the metre. The same may be done even in prose, when it conduces to the harmony of the period: thus, for செய்ய *to*

---

* On this point grammarians differ. Beschi here follows Vírasózhiyam (சந்இபய டௌம - அ, பா - இ) and Yápparungalam, as quoted in other grammars; while in Tonnûl Vil'accam, (எ சூ த. ஐச, ரூ த.) he follows Nannûl, (எ சூ த. எ சூ த இ ய ை - சஐச. ரூ த.) where the time allotted to abbreviated ஈ is only one மாத்இணா. The following verse from Náladiyár, is at variance with the latter authority.

> வைகஇழ் மலைவகல்வாரககண்டு ம்இன் துணரார்
> வைகஇழ் மலைவகல்வைவருடெமன் தின புறுவர்
> வைகஇழ் மலைவக றடமவாரூணடெம விஐவைவருதல்
> வைகவல்வைத்துணராதர்

அ - எ - கூ ம - கவி,

Although they daily see the morning break, yet they understand it not, and daily rejoice in the thought that the present day is the past one : they do not daily consider the past day to be one day added to that portion of their life which has expired.

do we may read செயல; for கொளல, கொளல *to buy*; for என்ன *what,* என; for என்ன *if said,* என்ன; for எல்லாம் *all,* எலாம; for உள்ளம் *heart,* உளம; &c. Thus also.

சொலஇதயார்க்குமெளியுயரியவாரு
சொலியவனைரு சசெயல

திருவ - சுயவ, அதி - ச, குற.

If the author had written செய்யல, the first syllable would have been long, and would not have suited the metre. The meaning of the couplet is: to *teach is easy to all; the difficulty is, to practice what we are taught.* This rule is, however, to be applied with caution; particularly where there is room for ambiguity: thus, if for வில்லை, the accusative of வில், *a bow,* you write விலை, the word will signify *price;* and if for கல்லை, the accusative of கல், *a rock,* you put கலை, the meaning will be *a stag* &c. The principal use of this rule is, to apprize the student, that many words, thus contracted, will be found in books, which must not be sought for in the dictionary under that form.

VI. Of the changes which take place in connecting the words of a Tamil sentence, I have spoken at length in the other grammar; but I think it necessary to make a few additional remarks in this.

First. If a word beginning with ந be preceded by a long monosyllable ending in ம, or by a polysyllable terminating with that letter, the ம of the first word is sunk, and the ந of the second remains unaltered: thus, for நாமநடந்த we must write நாநடந்த, and for மனமநோக, மனநோக. If the ம were not dropped, these words would be read *námanadanda, manamanóga.*

If the preceding word ending in ம be a short monosyllable, as செம, எம, இவம, the ம is changed to ந: thus, செம and நெல become செந்நெல *red paddy;* எம and நாடு, எந்நாடு *our country* or *what country;* and இவம and நீர், இவந்நீர் *hot water.* Hence, it is an error to write செனனெல, எனனீர், எனநூடு: this last word, thus written would signify *my country;* whereas எந்நாடு means either *our country,* or *what country?*

Secondly. If a word beginning by ந be preceded by a short monosyllable ending in ண or ன, the ந is changed to the preceding letter: thus,

தண் (from தண்மை, *cold*) and நீர் (*water*) become தண்ணீர் *cold water:* and கண் and நீர், கண்ணீர் *a tear.* So, from எல் and நாடு is formed என்னாடு *my country;* and from பொன் and நாணி, பொன்னாணி *a golden string.* The words thus united contain a double letter, which according to a rule laid down in No. 8, we may occasionally write single: thus, for கண்ணீர் we may use கணீர்; and for கண்ணல்லாள், கண்ணல்லாள் *a woman with good eyes.* We must be careful, however, not to write கணநல்லாள்; for that would be read *kananallál.*

If a word beginning with ந be preceded by a long monosyllable ending in ஐ or ஏ, or by a polysyllable terminating with either of those letters, the ந is dropped; thus வீண் and நசை form வீணசை *fruitless desire;* and நான் and நடந்தேன், நானடந்தேன் *I walked.* So also with polysyllables: thus, if the following words, அரசன் *king,* மன்னன் *monarch,* மகன் *son,* அரண் *fortification* கவண் *sling,* be united with the word நல்லன் (*masc.*) or நல்லது (*neu.*) they will form, respectively, அரசனல்லன், மன்னனல்லன், மகனல்லன், அரணல்லது, கவணல்லது. When, however, the last syllable of the polysyllable is short, the ந is sometimes changed to the preceding letter: thus, இவன் நாடு, இவனனாடு *his country;* மகன் நல்லன், மகனனல்லன்; அரண் நல்லது, அரணனல்லது. But we must never write இவனாடு; for this would be pronounced *ivanádu.*

Thirdly. If a word beginning with ந be preceded by one ending in ல், the ல் and ந are resolved into ன்; and if by one ending in ள், the ள் and ந are resolved into ண். In either case, the new letter is doubled, or not, according to the rule laid down in the foregoing paragraph: in other words, whenever the ந is permuted there, the ன or ண must be doubled here; and when the ந is struck out there, the ன or ண must remain single here: thus நல் *good* and நூல் *science* are resolved into நன்னூல் *belles lettres,* நால் and நான்கு into நான்னான்கு *four times four;* விரல் and நீண்டது into விரனீண்டது *the finger is extended;* thus, also, தென் and நீர் become தெண்ணீர் *clear water;* தாள் and நல்லாள், தாணல்லாள் *a woman with handsome feet,* and இருள் and நீக்கினன், இருணீக்கினன் *he dissipated the darkness.*

When a word ending with ஸ் comes before a word beginning with ம, the ஸ் is changed to ன் ; and when a word ending in ன் comes before such a word, the ன் is changed to ண்: thus, from கால and முகம is formed நான்முகம் *four faces;* and from பொருள and மாட்சி, பொருளுமாட்சி *the excellence of a thing.* Hence, the compound word பனைமை *plural* comes from பல் ; நனமை *goodness* from நல்; வெணமை *whiteness* from வெள; &c.

Fourthly. If a word beginning with த be preceded by one ending in ண், the த is changed to ட ; and if by one ending in ன், to ற ; and to this rule there is no exception: thus, கண், and துடைத்தான become கண்டு டைத்தான *he wiped his eye,* கவண் and தெரிந்தான, கவண்டெரிந்தான *he selected a sling.* If we were to omit the change, and write கவண்தெ ரிந்தான, the words would be read *kavanaterindán:* thus also, எனதல் must be written எனறல் *my head;* மானதல், மானறல், *a stag's head;* and இவனதல், இவனறல் *this man's head.*

When the word ending in ண் or ன், that precedes another beginning with த, is nominative in form, but oblique in signification, the ண் or ன் also may be changed to ட or ற, respectively, these letters being written, or dropped at pleasure. Agreeably to this rule, the author of சிந்தாமணி uses அவறேர், *his chariot* with single ற, for அவனேர் ; and he might also have written அவற்றேர்: thus, for விண்டிசை, *the region of heaven,* மண்டிசை, *the region of earth,* we may write விட்டிசை, மட்டிசை.

Tamil writers frequently employ the nominative for the accusative: in order, therefore, to distinguish the two, when the word which is thus used ends in ண் or ன், and is followed by another beginning with any rough letter, ண் must be changed to ட, and ன் to ற : thus, in the following instances, where மகன் *son* is put for மகனை, we write மகறேடிஞன், *he sought his son:* மகற்கண்டான *he saw his son:* மகற்சினந்தான, *he rebuk-ed his son:* மகற்பேணிஞன *he cherished his son.*

Fifthly. When a word beginning with த is preceded by one ending in ன் or ல், under such circumstances that, according to the rules of the common Tamil, (see the other grammar, No. 19. 20.) the த would be doubled, then, in this dialect, the த is not doubled, but the ன் in the one case is changed to ட், and the ல், in the other, to ற்; and it is then optional, whether to change the following த to the letter which precedes it, or to drop it: thus, in this dialect, we do not write நாள்த்தோறும், but நாட்டோறும் or நாடோறும்; *daily* neither வனத்தில்த்திரிந்தான், but வனத்திற்றிரிந்தான், or வனத்திறிரிந்தான், *he wandered in the forest.* A mode analogous to this is observed when any other of the rough letters follows ள் or ல், under the circumstances mentioned above: thus, instead of நாள்பட, we write நாட்பட *for a length of time*, thus, likewise நாட்கடன் *the duty of the day*, நாட்சிறிது, *days are few*; வனத்திற்சென்றான் கிடந்தான் - புக்கான் *In the forest he went, lay, entered.*

When, after a word ending in ள் or ல், a rough letter is not doubled in common Tamil, if the letter be த, it is often, according to this rule, changed to ட or ற; the preceding ள் or ல் also being sometimes changed to ட or ற, but more commonly dropped: thus, for இவள்தந்தாள், *She gave*, இவடந்தாள்; for குரல்தாழ்ந்தது - குராறுழ்ந்தது *the voice is low.*

Example.

அகழ்வாரைத்தாங்குநிலம்போலத்தம்மை
யிகழ்வார்ப்பொறுத்தறலை

திருவ - ௱௫௧, அதி - முதல், குற.

The two last words are put for பொறுத்தல்தலை. The passage is rendered: *It is a chief virtue to forgive slanderers, even as the earth supports those who cut it with the plough.*

Sixthly. Under what circumstances the rough letters க. ச. த. ப. are to be doubled at the beginning of a word, has been explained in the other grammar. I shall here add one rule: When a noun ending in ர் has the force of an accusative, but the nominative form, the rough letter which follows it must be doubled: thus, in the example just quoted, the construction is the same as if it were இகழ்வாரைப்பொறுத்தல்; but as the author has used the nominative இகழ்வார் for the accusative, he has written ப்பொறுத்தல், doubling the ப. If, without doubling this letter, he had written இகழ்வார்பொறுத்தல், the word இகழ்வார் would have been in the nominative; a construction which would have implied that the slanderers themselves were the persons to forgive.

CHAP. II.

OF THE NOUN.

OF THE DECLENSION OF NOUNS SUBSTANTIVE.

VII. Before I proceed to the forms of the cases by which nouns substantive are declined, I must observe that in the declension of nouns of this language, both in the common and in the superior dialect, there is a certain peculiarity. Beside the nominative form proper to each noun, and beside the terminations of cases in both numbers, common to all nouns, there is yet another termination or form, which I shall denominate *the oblique*. This is not the uninflected noun, neither is it any case of it ; for it differs from the nominative form, and is frequently used by itself, without any casual termination. The form of the oblique is not the same in all nouns, but varies according to the following rules.

First. All nouns, except those in அம், and some of those in உ, (of which hereafter,) form their oblique by adding இன் to the nominative : thus நா makes நாவின், *the tongue,* நமபி - நமபியின், *a lad,* தீ - தீயின், *fire,* மார்பு - மார்பின், *the breast,* கோண்மு - கோணமுவின், *a cloud,* மலை - மலை யின், *a mount,* கோ - கோவின், *a king,* So also, கண - கணணின், *the eye,* பொன - பொனனின், *gold,* பொய - பொயயின், *a lie,* அமர் - அமரின், *a battle,* பகல் - பகலின், *the day,* புகழ - புகழின், *praise,* தாள - தாளின், *the foot.*

If the final ன் be followed by a rough letter, it is changed to ற் ; as அழ கியகணணிற்குழவி, *a child with fine eyes.* Here, the termination இன் is by no means a form of the genitive ; for, in the higher dialect, this case ends in அது ; nor would the use of the genitive, in this instance, have been proper : but it is a form common to all the cases ; for, as we shall shortly see, it may take any of the casual terminations.

Secondly. All the nouns of which we have hitherto spoken, have another form of the oblique, which is the same as the nominative : accordingly the example last quoted might have been அழகியகண்குழவி ; or, more elegantly அழகியகட்குழவி : thus, also, பகிற்போசனம், or பகற்போ சனம, *a mid-day repast.*

Thirdly. Words ending in அம், to form the oblique, reject this termination, and take the affix அத்து : thus, மனம - மனத்து, *mind,* இடம - இடத்து *place.* To this last form we may add இன், dropping the உ : thus, மனத்தின, இடத்தின. Example, அழகியமுகத்திற்குழவி, or அழ கியமுகததுககுழவி ; *a child of a beautiful countenance.*

Fourthly. Of nouns in உ such as have for their final syllable டு or து, not preceded by a single consonant, but either by more than one syllable, as in தகடு *a plate,* கயறு *rope,* or by one long one, as in வீடு *house,* ஆறு *river,* form their oblique by doubling the ட or ற of their final syllable : thus, the foregoing words become தகட்டு, கயற்று, வீட்டு, ஆற்று, respectively. To these also, dropping the உ, இன் may be added : thus, தக ட்டின, கயற்றின, வீட்டின, ஆற்றின. Example : வீட்டுகதவு, or வீட்டிற்கதவு ; *the door of a house.*

VIII. The rules respecting the oblique should be carefully observed ; for it is very frequently employed in this dialect, it's uses are :

First. in declining nouns ; of which hereafter.

Secondly. In forming adjectives from nouns : thus, காட்டுவழி, or காட் டினைவழி : *A silvan road.*

Thirdly. To denote possession as பூணினமார்பன், or பூணமார்பன ; *A man having an ornament on his breast ;* பெரும்பொருளிற்சாததன, or பெரும்பொருட்சாததன, *Sáttan who possesses great wealth.*

Fourthly. In expressing the qualities of the mind, or the members of the body : thus, பெருநடையையிற்சாததன *Sáttan who has much kindness,* அருசாமனத்துசசாததன *Sáttan who has a fearless mind,* அகன்றமார் பிற்சாததன *the wide breasted Sáttan* கொடுமுகத்துசசாததன *the savage faced Sáttan.*

Fifthly. In expressing the time in which any person or thing exists or has existed, or in which any thing is or was done : as முற்காலத்துச்செ யதி, *the history of former time* இகாட்டபயிர் or இகாலிற்பயிர *the corn of this time.*

Sixthly. In expressing the place of abode as, இவ்வூர்ப்பசு *a cow of this village,* காட்டுப்பசு *a wild cow,* கொம்பூப்பூ *a flower growing on a branch,* குளத்தப்பூ *a flower growing in a tank.*

Seventhly. The oblique in தது is used for the ablative in இல் ; as அந்த தாததுயா முளினஉேறாம *we live in the world* for அந்தாததில்—அறிவாரில் விகில்லதது *there are none on earth able to know,* for நிலததுல். It is used also in comparison : thus, in the work entitled Silappadicàram we have அறைறவாயசூஞ்சததரு நநிகயர்கரும *the foot path on the declivity of the hill branches off like a trident,* where சூலதது is put for சூலதை தப ேபால. So also, மாவிததாஉததுமணிநிணாததது; *the gems are arranged according to the beauty of a garland;* where தாமதது is put for தாமதைத படேபால or தாமததாடில்.

We have stated, that the oblique has sometimes the same form as the nominative. In these cases, if it end with a vowel, or with ம or ர, and be followed by a rough letter, this last must be doubled, thus மலைப்பசு, *a mountain cow* கொடிப்பூ, *the blossom of a creeper* நெய்க்குடம *a pot of clarified butter* மலர்த்ேதன, *the honey of a flower;* if it end in ன் or ண், this letter must be changed to ட் ; and if in ன் or ல் to ற் : thus, எரி கட்சாததன, *The fiery eyed Sáttan* நெடுமவாட்சாததன, *Sáttan with a long sword* பொற்கம்பி, *gold wire* கடற்றிணை *a wave of the Sea.*

IX   I now proceed to the declension of the noun.

Pavananti, in his Nannùl, exhibits the cases, which he terms ேவற்று உைம, in the following method and order.

ெபயேரா - ஐ - ஆல் -
கு - இன - அது - கண -
விளி - ெயன றுகும
அவற றின ெபயர்குைற

ெசால்லதி - ெபயரியல் - நஉ௫ - ௫த.

This arrangement, although it differs from the European, I think it advisable to follow; because Tamil authors constantly distinguish the cases by number, as *the first, the second, the third,* case; which will not be understood, unless we know the order in which they are classed.

1st case. பெயர் *the name* or *nominative.*

2nd case, ஐ. This corresponds with our *accusative*, and is formed by adding the termination ஐ to the oblique: thus, from மலை *mount* மலை யின, or மலையை; from மனம் *mind* மனத்தினை or மனத்தை ; from வீடு, *house* வீட்டினை or வீட்டை; from ஆறு, *river* ஆற்றினை or ஆற்றை; from தகடு, *plate* தகட்டினை or தகட்டை; from கயறு rope கயற்றினை, or கயற்றை.

3d case, ஆல்; of which Pavananti says;

மூன்றுவத்து இருபால்ான்டுஒடாடு

கருவிகருத்தாவுடனிகழ்வதன பொருள

சொல்லதி. பெயரியல - சய், ரூத.

He here assigns, to this case four terminations; ஆல், ஆன், ஓடு, (with the first syllable long,) ஒடு, (with the first syllable short:) so that, we may say கண்ணால், கண்ணான், கண்ணோடு, கண்ணொடு, பார்த்தான், *he saw by,* or *with his eye ;* We may also add these terminations to the oblique, and use கண்ணினால், கண்ணினான், &c. When the termination ஒடு (with the first syllable short,) is used, the உ cannot be struck out: I have met with only one instance where this was done, which was in the poem Chintámani.

This case corresponds with our ablative, whether causal or social. First it expresses the active, material, and instrumental causes which are signified by the term கருவி - as; குயவருால்யகுடட, *a pot made by a potter,* மண ராால்யகுடம், *a pot made of earth,* திிகையால்யகுடம். *a pot made by means of a wheel.*

Secondly It expresses the impelling cause, whether extrinsick, as the command of an other, or intrinsick, as the final design: these are signified

---

Note. The affix ஒடு which generally designates the social is used for the causal, where the cause and effect are co-existent. as தீயொடுபுகை, *smoke from fire* பஞ்யாற்கு ளிர், or பனியொடுகுளிர், *cold from dew.*

by the term கருத்தா, as அரசனைஆயகுளமை, *a tank made by command of the king;* பயிறிஒ லாய குளம, *a tank made for the purpose of agriculture.*

Thirdly, it expresses connexion, which is termed உடனிகழ்வு, and it then answers to the social ablative.

4th case, கு. This corresponds with our *dative.* Examples: மகைக்கு, or மகையிறகு; முகததுககு, முகததிறகு

5th case, இல், or இன. Respecting this case, The Nannûl states.

ஐந்தாவததறகுருபில்லுமினறு
நீகுடுலாய பெல்கையெதடுபபொருளே.

சொலெதி. பெயரியல் - சஉ, ரூத.

The forms of the fifth case are இல் *and* இன, *they import removal, similitude, limit or cause.*

As the termination இன is also one of the forms of the oblique, we shall often find it doubled; the first இன being the termination of the oblique, and the second that of the 5th case: thus, மகையில், or மகையின, மகையினில், or மகையினின. This case is used as follows.

First; to express நீகுகல் *motion from a place as,* வீடடினிககினன, *He departed from the house.* thus,

தலையினினழ்ந்ததமயிரவணயராமாகதா
நிலயினினழ்ந்தககடை

இருவ - கூய்சு, அடி - ச, குற.

As hair fallen from the head, so are men who have fallen from their station to low estate. This force of the 5th case accounts for its use in comparison, of which we have spoken in the other grammar; for, அதனிறபெரிதிது signifies literally, *quitting that, this is to be reckoned great.* The same with the superlative; for, செல்வஙகளிற செல்வம signifies literally, *Rejecting all other blessings, this is to be deemed a blessing;* that is, the best blessing.

Secondly, to express *similitude,* ஒபபு: as மினனிளெழியுமினபய, for மினவைபொல்வொழியுமினபம; *pleasure vanishes like lightning.* Thus, the celebrated author of Chintàmani, describing the road which led to a certain mountain, says;

செல்வர்மனத்திஜெஙகிததிருவினமாகதர்டெஞசின
எல்வகியிருவி்ஞறஙகிபபுஙதாஜிவி்ஙடெஞுழுஙகிக
டொல்லுமாவினமயஙகிசசி ஞியார்டொகாணடெொடார்பிற
செல்வசடெசல்லவஙகுடெஞஞிடெசஙகில்லமபுசெசர்நதான

டெகமசரியாஙிலமமடகம - ௫.ம.கவி.

In this single stanza, the case இன is used no less than five times, to express similitude. To shew this more clearly, I will translate it into common Tamil. செல்வஙகளையுடையொர்மனததைபடெபால்டெமடெஙழுஙடெததஙி தஙாஙிததொர் டெஙஞசைப டெபால்பபகஇம்ருணடஙாகிய பூவிதழ டெமதுலைவப டெபால்டெமடெயபனளஞுஙின ஞிசசங்ததகடெகால்இமபாமணைபபடெபால்க டெகாணி படெபாயசெஞஞிஙைகதைதபடெபால்ப டெபாகபடெபாகககுஞஙதுவருமவழியா ஞடவலையசடெஞஞதான். *He approached the mountain by a road soaring as the mind of the wealthy, dark at midday as the heart of the indigent, level as the petals of a flower, winding like a deadly serpent, lessening in progress as the friendship of the mean.*

Thirdly; to express எல்லை, a limit; thus இருககாவஇஙினடெஞஙஙுகஙா விஙியாஞு *The river Càviri bounds Tirucàvalùr to the south.*

Fourthly; to express எது, cause; thus டெபானினுயருடடம, *a pot made of gold,* டெபாருளிடெனனியன, *a man poor in substance* அஞததிஞடெபஙியன, *a man of exalted virtue.*

6th. case, அது. This corresponds exactly with our *genitive.* Respecting this case, we find in Nannùl, the following remark:

அஞடெஞருமைகைததுவுமாதுவுமடனைமைகககவுஙுருபாம;

டெஞால்எஇ. டெபயஙியல - சங, ௬த.

The termination of the 6th case is அது *or* அத *for the singular, and* அ *for the plural:* the meaning of which is, that the singular or plural termination is to be affixed to the noun in the genitive, not according as this is singular or plural, but according as the noun, which governs that genitive, is singular or plural. Thus, with the governing noun in the singular; வாழையது பழங; *the fruit of a plantain tree* யாவணையது கடஙஙடம, *a herd of elephants;* மஙததின துடெகாமபு *the branch of a tree;* டெஙல்லது, *or*

நெல்லினது சோறு, *boiled rice of paddy*; எனது, or எழுது, நினது or திருது - நிலம *the land of me, or thee*, with the governing noun in the plural; என்கைகள *the hands of me*, தன்யாவணகள *the elephants of him*, குதிணயமயிர்கள *the hairs of a horse*.

The plural termination is also employed though the governing noun be in the singular, provided it be used in a plural sense: thus speaking of both hands, I may say, என்கை *my hands*, உன்கை *thy hands*, Example.

நுன்சிறடிடநோவவநடநதுசேடெல
ஒல்ன்தாவியகததுறைவாடெயனுநீ

சிநதாமணி, கேமசரியாநிலமபகம - நாசூ, கவி.

Weary not thy delicate feet by departing hence, thou who art the inmate of my soul. Here, the word அடி being singular, the author writes எனதாவி, but அடி, although in the singular, has a plural sense; and he therefore writes நுன்சிறடி. The metre shews that we should read *nuna*, not *nun*. Observe, that துன்து and நினது may both be put for உனது, as will be explained in the proper place.

The genitive case is however seldom used, the oblique form being employed in its stead: thus, காட்டகத்தில for காட்டினதகத்தில *in the desert*; மனசதுறுதி for மனததினதுறுதி *the firmness of mind*. The *word* உடைய, which serves for a genitive termination in common Tamil must not be so employed here: in fact, it is not a casual termination, but an adjective, regularly formed from the substantive உடை, according to rules which will hereafter be given.

7th. case, கண: &c. This corresponds with the local ablative. கண, however, appears rather to be a word which forms a compound with the noun, than a casual termination; and although the original meaning is *eye*, it here signifies *place*. In confirmation of this remark, we find it expressly stated in Nannûl rule 45, that we may use, in the same way, any word importing *place*; such as தகி, கடை, இடை, முன, பின, வடெ, இடம, கீழ, டிடல, உன, புறடெ, புடை, உளி, உழி,

with many others. (*) Of these words, such as terminate in ம must be used in the oblique form தது: thus, காட்டிற கண, or காட்டிடத்து, காட்டகத்து, காட்டிற புறத்து *in the desert* &c. It follows that, as இல is a word meaning *place*, or habitation, it, likewise, may be employed in forming this case: in fact, it is so used in common Tamil: thus, மலையில *in the mount*, முகத்தில *in the face:* the termination இல, therefore, serves for two cases, the fifth and the seventh. When கண is used in forming the 7th case, the ண must be changed to ட, if the following word commence with a rough letter: thus மலைகட்புலி *a tyger in the mount*, வயறகட்குரு *a heron in a paddyfield*, பொர்ற கடகிளி *a parrot in a grove*, அறவோர்கட்சுகம *happiness is with the virtuous*, அரசர்கட்டிரு *wealth is with kings.*

From the foregoing remarks it appears, that, wherever, in common Tamil, the expression கிட *near, at,* is used, we may, in this dialect, employ the case கண: thus, அவனகட்சென்றேன *I went to him*, ஊரின கடகணடேன *I saw him near the village* &c. Example,

நல்லார்கட்பட்டவறுமையினின்றுத
கல்லார்கட்பட்டடிரு

திருவ - சக - அதி - அ, று.

Wealth with the ignorant is worse than poverty with the wise. Here, the locality is designated in English by *with.*

With respect to the word உள், I take this occasion to remark, that, as it is included among those words which designate *place*, it cannot correctly be used, as it commonly is, with a dative; but requires to be coupled with the oblique; thus, அறத்தள or அறத்தி இள, *in virtue* வீட்டுள ஷேன, or வீட்டி இனஷேன *in a house* அவற்றுள, or அவற்றி இள *in them.*

(*) The whole of these words are enumerated in the following rule of Nannúl.

கண - கால் - ஏடை - இடை - தவி - வாய - திசை - வயின -
முன - சார் - வலம - இடம - மேல் - கீழ - புற - முதல் -
பின - பாடு - அகில - தேம - உழ - வழி - உளி - உழி -
உள - அகம - புறம - இல் - இடபொருளுருவே
பெயரிய ஷ - சரு - கூத.

8th case, விளிவேற்றுமை, *the vocative.* Having enlarged on the formation of this case in the other grammar, and the remarks made there, being equally applicable here, I shall, without repeating them, proceed to notice certain peculiarities of this dialect.

First. In Nannùl, (Rule 46, Chap. on the noun,) we are told, that the vocative is either இயல்பு, the simple nominative, or is formed in the following ways: by குறறல், *elision;* by மிகுதல், *augmentation;* by ஈற நினறிரிபு, *the change of the last letter;* by ஈறறயறநிரிபு, *the change of the penultimate;* or by some of these ways combined: thus, இயனவாழி, *farewel Sir;* where the simple nominative is used; இயவாழி, where the letter ன is dropped; இயனேவாழி, where the nominative is augmented by the letter ெ; இயஓவ, where the final ன is changed to ஓவ; இயா னவாழி, where the penultimate is changed from a short to a long letter; இயாவாழி, where the last letter is dropped, and the last but one changed; (†) and இயாஓவ, and இயாஓவா, where, in each word, the last letter, and the last but one, are changed.

Secondly. Nouns masculine ending in ஆன, besides the modes explained in the other grammar, form their vocative, either by அனஓபடை, as, பெருமான *king,* voc. பெருமாஅன; (‡) or by changing the final ன to ய, as, கிரியான *a mountaineer,* voc. கிரியாய, உணடான *an eater,* voc. உணடாய, நெடுநகையான *a man with long arms,* voc. நெடு நகையாய. To this vocative we may also add ெ thus, கிரியாஓய *O mountaineer,* உணடாஓய *O eater.* (§) &c. This last mode is used more especially with appellative nouns, of which hereafter.

(†) Thus, also, இஓய, where the final ன is dropped, and the penultimate changed to ெ. See நனநூல், சொல்லதி, பெயரியல - ரூ, சூத.

(‡) உயர்திணை words ending in ன may also form the vocative by changing the final ன to ஓ thus, பெருமான voc. பெருமாஓவா, *O king.* See நனநூல், சொ லதி, பெயரியல - ரூ, சூத.

(§) Appellatives in ஆன may also form the vocative by changing the ஆ of this form into ஓ, thus, உணஓடாஓய, *O eater;* வாயிஓலாஓய, *O porter.*

See நனநூல், சொரலதி, பெயரியல - ரூ, சூத.

Thirdly. Nouns masculine and feminine ending in எ preceded by a long syllable, may likewise form their vocative by அனெபெடை : thus கேஅன *a name of the god of love*, voc. கேஅஎன. If the long syllable preceding எ contain the vowel அ, the vocative is formed by dropping the எ, thus, கணளுஎன, voc. கணளு ; to which we may add ய, கணளுய. If the syllable before எ be short, the vocative may be formed by changing the short penultimate to its corresponding long letter; and this serves also for the vocative neuter: thus, மகஎ *children*, voc. மகாஎன, நமர்கஎ *our people*, நமர்காஎன, இஉகஎ *moon*, இஉகாஎன, இளிகஎ *parrot* இளிகாஎன. If the vowel in the short syllable be அ, it is sometimes changed to எ long; but this form will not serve for the neuter: thus, அடிகஎ, which is the same with சுவாமி *Lord*, voc. அடிகேஎ, Examples. தவமிஃது தொகாவெடயெமடி கேஎ — எற்றுமடிகேளுஎஎன, that is *We worship thee, O Lord.*

Fourthly. Nouns masculine and feminine, ending in ர் preceded by a long syllable, may form their vocative by அனெபெடை, thus, தமிமார் *younger brothers*, voc. தமிமஎஅர். If the vowel preceding ர் be அ this may be changed to ஈ thus, உளாரர் *villagers*, voc. உளரீர் ; to which we may add எ, உளரீகே,—so also from சானேறுர் *the learned*, சானநீர், சானநீகே. If the ர் be preceded by அ, this is changed either into இ or ஈ, thus, தெவவர் *enemies*, voc. தெவவீர் வெகதர் *kings*, வெகஈர், பாகர் *charioteers* பாகீர்: or, the original word may remain unchanged, and எர் be added; thus, கமர் *our men*, voc. கமரீர், பிறர் *foreigners*, voc. பிறரீர். If the ர் be preceded by இயர், the யர் is dropped, the இ is changed to ஈ and எ is added : thus நமியியர் *lads*, voc. நமிஈகே, தமியியர் *younger brother*, voc. தமிஈகே. Even words which do not end in ர் but have their singular in இ, may form their vocative plural by the addition of எர் or எகே: thus தமி *younger brother*, voc. தமிஈர், or தமிஈகே; சாமி *lord*, voc. சாமிஈர், or சாமிஈகே. Lastly: certain neuter nouns, when used in token of love or joy, assume the masculine or feminine form, as I shall hereafter explain: thus, the words மயிலனர் *those who resemble peacocks*, and குயிலர் *those who resemble cocilas*, may be used instead of மயிகஎ *peacocks*

குயில்கள் *cocilas* under the foregoing rules, their vocatives will then become, மயிலீரோ, குயிலீரோ, respectively.

Fifthly. Nouns masculine and feminine, ending in ல், or ய், preceded by a long syllable, may form their vocative by அளபெடை: thus, மால் *a name of Vishnu*, voc. மாஅல்; thus, a certain poet has, வலம்புரித்தடக கைமாஅல் *O mighty handed Vishnu*: so also, பூணய *a woman adorned with jewels*, voc. பூணஅய. But if அ, which is a short vowel, precede ல், the vocative is formed by changing that vowel into ஆ thus, தோன றல் *a son or king*, voc. தோனறூல், மடவரல் *a woman*, voc. மடவரால். The same with nouns neuter; thus, ஓங்கல், *a mountain,* தூங்கல், *an elephant,* voc. ஓஉகால், தூஉகால்.

Sixthly. In Nannûl, Rule 56, we are told, that the vocative formed by அளபெடை is used only in calling to persons at a distance, while that which is formed by dropping the final letter, as well as that which has the same form as the nominative, is used only in addressing those who are near; that the vocative formed by adding ஓ, is used only in exclamations of pain or lamentation; and that the remaining forms are used indifferently.

SECTION THE SECOND.
OF NOUNS APPELLATIVE.

X. Appellative nouns are called in Tamil பகுபதம், in contradistinction to nouns proper, which are termed பகாபபதம். பதம் signifies *a word* பகு, for பகும், the future participle from the verb பகுத்தல் *to divide or to be divisible*, signifies *divisible, consisting of parts, one composed of several;* பகா, the negative participle from the same verb, means *indivisible* or *simple*. The Deity may be called பகாபபொருள *a being simple or uncompounded;* and created things, பகுபொருள *compounded beings.*

Nouns proper are called பகாபபதம் *simple words,* because they refer to one object only. The word வில், for instance, is பகாபபதம், because it refers to one object, *a bow.* Nouns appellative are called பகுபதம், compound words, because they refer to two objects: thus, if we form an appellative from the word வில், as வில்லாளன *a bow man,* this refers to two objects, the bow itself, and the man who holds it.

To the foregoing definition it may be objected, that the word வில், for instance, is what is termed திரிசொல் *a simple word with more than one meaning*; and that, from the variety of its significations, as *light, coral, anemone, a mast,* &c. it cannot properly be termed பகாபபதம். But this is of no consequence: because it has more than one meaning only when considered singly, (hence திரிசொல்,) (‡) and not when it is regarded in conjunction with its appellative, for the word வில்லாளன, *a bow man,* for instance, fixes the meaning of வில், when considered as its proper noun. This remark will be found to apply with equal justice to any other appellative noun.

XI. In this dialect, appellatives are formed at pleasure from any noun or verb. The primitives from which they are formed, are referred to six heads, called *common places,* பொதுவிடம். In Nannúl, (Part the first,

---

(‡) In Nannúl, the definition of திரிசொல் is as follows :

ஒருபொருளுக்குறித்ததபலசொல்லாகியும

பலபொருளுக்குறித்ததொருசொல்லாகியும.

அரிதுணர்ப்பொருளன திரிசொல்லாகும

சொல்லதிகாரம், பெயரியல் - ௴ - ௲.

When one object is expressed by many words or one word designates many objects, the object difficult of apprehension, becomes a திரிசொல்.

Hence, it signifies either *a synonyme,* or *a word with several meanings,* thus, மலை, வெற்பு, கிரி, all which signify *a mountain,* are each a திரிசொல், in the former sense ; and காகம், which signifies *a monkey, a snake, a mountain,* &c. is a திரிசொல் in the latter.

Chap. II. Rule 5.) these are thus enumerated: பொருளிடங்காலருகிவிண குணகவிதாத்கின் வருபகுபதமே.

First, பொருள *a thing possessed*, as விலவிினன *a bowman*, from விஸ; முடியிினன *one who wears a crown*, from முடி. Second, இடம *place*, as மலையிினன *a mountaineer*, from மலை; தெலுஙகன *a Telinga man*, from தெலுஙகு. Third, காலம *time*, as இககாலததான *a man of the present time*, முறகாலததான *one of former times*, பாளியான, கெடலையான, *one born under the constellation.* பாளி *or* கெடலை. Fourth, சிவய *a component part*, as தொளைகாததன *a man with a long bored ear*, நெடுஙகணனன *one whose eyes are long*. Fifth, குணம *a property of mind* or *body*, as கொடியன *a cruel man*, from கொடுமை; இனியன *a mild man*, from இனி; கறியன *a black man*, from கருமை; கூனன *a hunch backed man*, from கூன; நெடியன *a long man*, from நெடுமை; குளனன *a short man*, from குளைவம. Sixth, தொழில *employment* or *action*, as வாணிகன *a merchant*, from வாணிகம; செலவிின *a traveller*, from செலவு; விரைவிினன *a quick man*, from விரைவு. To the sixth place belong also, ஒதினன - ஒதுவான - *a reader*, from the verb ஒததல; காததவன - காபபான *a preserver*, from the verb காததல, and the like; which, as has been stated in the other grammar, may be formed at pleasure: as such words, however, may be taken either for the third person of the verb, or for appellative nouns, we are told, in Nannúl, that a distinction is to be made in pronouncing them. When the word ஒதுவான, for instance, is an appellative noun, the ஒ is to be pronounced more open, than when it is part of the verb.

XII. Concerning the formation of appellatives from common places, I shall not venture to give any rules as invariable. Pavananti himself, in his Nannùl says, that this must be learned rather from the practice of ancient writers, than from precepts. So irregular, indeed, is the formation of appellatives, that it is impossible to fix it by any certain rules. For instance, from வில, *a bow*, are formed விலி, விலைன, விலலைவன, விலனொனன, விலைன, விலகிளன, all which signify *an archer*. Yet, from கண, we cannot, in the same way, form கணகி, for a masculine appellative, that word being used only for the feminine: neither from மகல, can we form மகலி, for either gender. I observe, however,

First. That we learn from Nannûl that appellatives are to be distinguished into two parts; பகுதி, the primitive from which the appellative is formed, and விகுதி the appellative termination; thus, in the appellative வில்லன், வில் is the பகுதி, and அன் the விகுதி. When appellatives are formed from nouns referrible to any of the common places but the fifth, the பகுதி, or root, (excepting nouns in அம், of which hereafter,) remains unaltered; the விகுதி, or appellative termination, being simply affixed to its nominative or oblique: thus, பூண் *an ornament*, app. பூணன், பூணி னன்; ஊர் *a village*, app. ஊரான்; நாள் *a day*, app. நாளினன்; கண் *an eye*, app. கணணன்; உணவு *food*, app. உணவினன்; in all which instances, the விகுதி is affixed without any change of the பகுதி.

But in forming appellatives from the fifth place குணம், the primitive noun undergoes a change: thus, the appellative from கொடுமை *cruelty*, is கொடியன், not கொடுமையன். So also கருமை *blackness*, app. கரியன்; நெ டுமை *length*, app. நெடியன்; புதுமை *novelty*, app. புதியன், பெருமை *greatness*, app. பெரியன்; நன்மை *goodness*, app. நல்லன்; வெண்மை *whiteness*, app. வெளன்.

Secondly. That விகுதி, the appellative termination, is generally, for the masculine singular, அன், அவன், ஆன், ஓன்; for the feminine singular, அள், ஆள், அவள், இ; for both genders in the plural, அர், ஆர், அவர்; for the neuter singular, அது, து; for the neuter plural, அவை, அன், அ.

These terminations are affixed to proper nouns under the fifth head in the manner already shewn: thus, from கொடுமை, are formed, for the masculine singular, கொடியன், கொடியவன், கொடியான், கொடியோ ன்; for the feminine singular, கொடியள், கொடியவள், கொடியாள்: (but not கொடியி, though we say நங்கி, &c.) for the plural of both genders, கொடியர், கொடியார், கொடியவர்; for the neuter singular, கொடிய து, கொடியது; for the neuter plural, கொடியவை, கொடியன், கொடிய. Such proper nouns belonging to the other five classes, as do not end in அம், form their appellatives, as already stated, by adding the terminations enumerated above, either to their nominative, or to the oblique:

(See VII.) thus, from the nominative வெறபு *a mountain*, are formed, வெறபன, வெறபயன, வெறபோன, வெறபான, &c. and from its oblique,வெறறின,are formed வெறறினன, வெறறினைவன, வெறறிஞன, வெறபிஜேஞன, &c. Thus, also, புஎன், app. புஎினன, &c. சசீ *filthiness*, app. சசீடன, &c. or, from its oblique சசீடடு, or ச-ஈடடன, app. சசீ டன, சசீடடினைன, &c. நாறி *a region*, app. நாடன; or, from its oblique நாடடு, or நாடடன, app. நாடடன, or நாடடினை : of these, the appellative formed from the oblique in டறி, is more elegant than that formed from the oblique in டடன. Again, from வயறு *the belly*, வய றன, or, more elegantly, from its obliques வயறறு, வயறறின, are formed வயறறன, வயறறினைன.

Thirdly. Nouns ending in அம form their appellative, either by changing the ம into ன, or எ; or by changing the அம into இ. The latter form is generally used for the feminine only, but sometimes for both genders; thus, தருமம *charity*, app. masc. தருமன, fem. தருமன, தருமி; காமம *lust*, app. masc. காமன, fem. காமன, காமி. But அஜகாரம *pride*, and உலோபம *covetousness* form அஜகாரி and உலோபி, for both genders.

The foregoing mode cannot, however, be used, when the proper noun consists of two short syllables: thus, அறம *virtue*, and மனம *mind*, cannot form அறன and மனன for their appellatives. The reason of this is, that, in the superior dialect, the greater part of such nouns may themselves terminate in ன, as well as in ம, so that அறம and அறன, மனம and மனன, are the same. This, however, is not always the case; we cannot, for instance, employ ஞனன instead of ஞனம. In the use of such words, we are told in Nannùl that the practice of ancient writers must be our guide.

The mode in which nouns in அம most frequently form their appellatives, is, by affixing the appellative terminations to their oblique: thus, மனம, obl. மனததறு or மனததின; the former of which, taking the several terminations, gives, for the singular masculine, app. மனததன, மனதத வன, மனததான, மனதஜேதான; for the singular feminine, மனததன, மன

நதவள, மனததாள, மணததி; for the plural of both genders, மணததர்,
மனததார், மனததவர்; for the singular neuter, மனததது; for the plural
neuter, மனததன், மன தத. The second form of the oblique gives மணத
இனஎ, மனததிஎவஎ, &c. Thus, also, தருமம, app. தருமததஎ, &c. கா
ஸம app. காலததினஎ, &c.

Fourthly. A few proper nouns in இ become appellative by the
addition of ஞர் or னர், and the letter ந, which is generally initial, is then
written in the middle of the word: thus, இஎஎ *a branch*, app. இஎஞர்,
or இஎநர் *relations by blood;* இஎஎ, app. இஎஞர், or இஎனர் *youths.*
This method is seldom used.

Fifthly. Respecting the formation of appellatives from verbs,
general rules are given in No. 106 of the other grammar. I have here
only to add, that appellatives, serving both for the masculine and feminine, are often formed from the neuter gender future, by changing the
உம into இ: thus, விழுஙதம, from விழுஙகல் *to devour*, app. விழுஙகி;
உணகுஅ, from உணஎல் *to eat*, app. உணகி; இனனும, from இனஎல் *to
eat*, app. இனனி; இடகதும, from இடததல் *to lay*, app. இடஎகி. From
some verbs, appellatives cannot be thus formed; the rule, therefore, is
not universal.

XIII. It has been stated, that the அதி, or appellative termination, for
the neuter plural, may be அ: thus, செ'டிய, அதிய, மனதத. Example.

செயநகரியசெயவார்பெரியர்சிநியர்
செயநகரியசெயகலாதார்

திருவ-ரு, அதி-கா, குந.

Things difficult of execution the great perform,
Low persons are not capable of mighty deeds.

Now, the word அதிய, for instance, may, from its termination, stand,
either for an adjective, (of which hereafter ;) as in அதியெ'ாருஎ *a difficult thing*, or for an appellative noun of the neuter plural; as in அதிய
செயவர். In the latter case, it is used somewhat like the words *difficilia,*

ardua, multa, &c. in Latin; which may be written either with the word *negotia,* or without it: as, *ardua negotia proponis,* or simply, *ardua proponis.* This observation must be carefully remembered; for, in this dialect, appellatives are formed from any noun, and the termination in question frequently occurs; thus, with தகை *good quality,* which signifies the same as குணம், we have தகையசெயதான; that is, குணதகைத புடை யயற்கைநசெயதான *he did acts of a good kind:* thus, also, மெயயபொருளவாகி; that is, மெயயபொருஙஙகிகொணடணைவாகி *those things becoming realities,* and இவையுனைபால்வெனறுன; that is, உனைபால்லாயினவெனறுன *he said, these things occurred before you.* Instances of this kind are constantly to be found in authors.

XIV. In this language there is a peculiarity, which, I believe, will not be found in any other. It is this, that, whilst appellatives in general are declined through all the cases, like nouns substantive, those which are formed either from the fifth head of primitives, or from the oblique of any noun whatever, are also conjugated through all the persons, like verbs. In this case, they are called விகைககுறிபபு, *the sign of the verb;* that is, nouns serving, like a verb, to express some action or passion: thus, வெறிவினைன *he dwells on a mountain.*

The following is an example of an appellative declined through all the cases, like a noun substantive: பூணினன, பூணினஊன, பூணைகாருல, பூணி னறகு, பூணினனின, பூணினனனது, பூணினனைகணை; all from பூணை.

The following is an appellative declined through all the persons, with the verbal terminations proper to this dialect; of which hereafter: நான பூணிடேனன, நீபூணிவன, அவனபூணினன, அவள பூணினன, அதுபூணிறறு; நாமபூணிடேனம, நீர்பூணினீர், அவர்பூணினர், ஆவைபூணின. When thus conjugated, they have the force of verbs, and form of themselves complete sentences. The foregoing examples, therefore, signify: *I have a neck-lace of gems, Thou hast a necklace of gems,* &c. Hence the following are complete sentences: இறைவகொடியை *O king! thou art cruel;* கவெலி ததாடேயயெனகளினைய *O virgin mother! how dear art thou to me!* The same when we apostrophize inanimate objects: நீசேதனனியை *O water!*

how cold thou art ! நீயெவெயகை *O fire, how hot thou art !* or when we simply state the fact : சீர்தணளிற்று *the water is cold;* தீயெயயது *the fire is hot.*

Hence we perceive the etymology of the word அடியேன, which is so frequently used. It is an appellative from the noun அடுமை *servitude,* and, as its termination implies, has the force of a verb, of the first person singular, and signifies, *I am a servant.* To use this word like a noun, as அடியேன, அடியேயண, அடியேனுல், அடியேனுகு, &c. is erroneous : for the noun is not அடியேன, but அடியன, அடியன ; or அடி யான, அடியான. Custom may sanction this error in the common dialect, but it is altogether inadmissible in this.

நல்ல, இல்ல, அவ்வ, and similar words, being appellatives, are conjugated, in this dialect, like verbs: thus, நான - நவ்வேன, இல்லேன, அவ்வேன ; நீகவ்வ் or நல்லாய, இல்வல் or இல்லாய, அல்வல் or அவ்வலா ய; அவன - நல்வன or நல்லான் &c. அவள - நல்வள or நல்லாள ; &c. அது நல்வது or நனது, இல்லது or இனது, அவ்வது or அனது; நாம - நவ்வேலம or நல்லனம, &c. நீர்கவ்வீர் &c, அவர்கவ்வர் or நவ்லார், &c. அவைநவ்வின் or நல்வ, இல்லன் or இல்வ, அவ்வன் or அவ்வ.

In common Tamil, when a person or thing which is produced, is not that which we want, we apply the word அவ்வ indiscriminately to either : as, நானவ்வ, நீயல்வ, அதால்வ, அதுகளல்வ. In this dialect, on the contrary, when we make a simple denial as to the essence of any person or thing, the word அவ்வ, must agree in gender with the object to which the negation refers : thus, நானவ்வேன *I am not the person,* இதனது இவ்வது *this is not the thing:* so நீரல்லீர், அவையவ்வ or அவ்வன : and when we make a negation respecting one person or thing, and an affirmation respecting another, the word அவ்வ must agree in gender with the object to which the affirmation refers : thus, I see something at a distance, but doubt whether it be a man or a horse; on ascertaining the point, I say, *it is not a horse, but a man ;* which must be rendered,

குஇனையல்லன் மனிதன ; and, if I make the affirmation respecting the horse, மனிதனனறுகுஇனா. With regard to the number of அல்லன, the principle of concordance is the same: thus, to express *there are not several men, but one*, I say, பல்லைல்லெஒருவன ; and vice versâ, ஒருவனல் ல்பலர். So likewise, if I deny that there are several things, but affirm that there is one, I say, பல்லையல்லஒதனனறு *there are not several, there is one*: and, vice versâ, ஒனறல்லபல்லை *there are several; not one only.*

The mode in which appellatives are conjugated must be carefully observed, as it will elucidate many passages, which would, otherwise, be extremely obscure. The following quotation contains several examples of the rules on this head. The stanza is of the kind called Viruttam but is to be read, as will hereafter be explained, with the same cadence as that termed Ven'bà.

சீஒல்லஎ குளளருடையை நீஇதல்லா நீஇதெஙளியை
நேஒல்லாமஇெவல்வினியைஇெஇகிகினியை   சீ
யாஇஒல்லஇெமையபாடிஇகளிஇஒெயஇே   ற்
பாஇஒல்லஇெமுனவஹைபபனியாஇதவாஇஒறன   ஙென

The appellatives உடையன, ஒளியன, வஇியன, இனியன, are here used as verbs, in the second person singular, உடையை, ஒளியை, வஇியை, இனியை. The stanza is rendered, *O Lord! thou hast all good within thee. Thou, who art exempt from all evil, appearest with splendour. Thou art omnipotent and without equal. Thou rejoicest the world. Who can declare all thy perfections? If thus it be, then, wherefore does all the world neglect to worship thee?*

XV. There is yet one remark, which, though it belongs more immediately to the conjugation of verbs, I shall introduce here, in order to complete the subject of appellative nouns.

Appellatives, when conjugated as verbs, are inflected with the regular verbal terminations, (of which in the proper place,) except in the third person singular of the neuter gender, which takes several forms, and terminates in அஇ, இஇ, றறு, or இ. It may be stated as a general rule, that the third person singular neuter may always take the termination அது: thus, மகிழ்ினது, உளரினது; but since this is likewise the termination of the sixth case, or genitive, it is seldom used, except in appellatives formed from the 5th class of primitives by altering or abbreviating the proper noun, as explained above: for, it then admits of no ambiguity: thus, கொடியது or கொடிது *it is cruel*, கரியது or கரிது *it is black*.

With regard to other appellatives the following rules are to be observed. First. Those derived from nouns ending in ஐ, ர், ய், form the third person neuter singular by adding the termination த்து to those nouns: thus, உடை *possession*, app. உடைத்து; தீமை *evil*, app. தீமைத்து; நடை *progress*, app. நடைத்து: thus, also, பெயர் *a name*, app. பெயர்த்து; ஊர் *a village*, app. ஊர்த்து; பொய *a lie*, app. பொய்த்து; மெய் *truth*, app. மெய்த்து, Example:

பல்லார்பகைகொளலிற்பதத்தித்தத்தீமைதஇே
நல்லார்தொடர்கைவிட

திருவ-சய்ரு, அதி-ய், குற.

Here தீமைத்து is the same as தீமையதாகும; *it is worse*. The passage is rendered: *To lose the friendship of the good is tenfold worse, than to be hated by the many.*

Secondly: those derived from the oblique in இன், form the appellative by changing the ன் to றது: as, விலகின, app. விலகிறது; பொறவின app. பொறவிறது, இருவின, app. இருவிறது: thus, in the verse quoted in P. 16, we have எல்லையிருளிறறுஇ &c.

Thirdly: those derived from nouns in ல், form it by changing the ல் to றது: thus, மேல் *above*, app. மேறது; முதல் First, app. முதறது; வெளில *heat*, app. வெளிறது: thus, a certain poet has பொருவெபொாழி வார்மேறெறுபுகழ, *Praise is heaped on those who pour forth their wealth*. Here, மேறெறுபுகழ has the force of மேலெெதபகழ.

Fourthly: those derived from nouns in ன், form the appellative by changing the ன் to ட்டு: thus, மாரிகான *winter*, app. மாரிகாட்டு; so that இபபயிர்மாரிகாட்டு is a complete proposition signifying, *this is a*

winter crop, or *this kind of cultivation is proper to the rainy season :* so
also அபயிர்கோடைநாட்டு *that is a summer crop,* or *that kind of cul-*
tivation is proper to the summer season : and, as ன் is changed to ட், (see
VI. 4,) a third person neuter singular is formed from கண, the sign of the
seventh case, by changing the ன் to ட்டு: in this form it becomes a verb,
and renders the sentence complete. Example.

அனைநிவுதேறநடிவாவினைமையிஙானகு
நனகுடையானகட்டுட்டெரி   வு

திருவ - ருமெ, அஇ - ௩, குற.

He who hath these four qualifications, loyalty, wisdom, decision,
disinterestedness, with him is perspicuity (of counsel) found. Here கட்டு
has the force of கணைதரம, (Lat. est opud) is with. The meaning is;
Love towards the king, skill in the law, decision of opinion, and disinte-
restedness, are four qualifications, with the possessor of which the best
counsel is found.

This rule shews, that the words இருட்டு and பொருட்டு which, in
common Tamil, have come to be used as nouns, are, in fact, appellatives,
of the third person singular neuter, from இருள and பொருள. We have
stated, in the other grammar, No. 107, that the third person neuter of
the preterite serves for a verbal noun: the third person neuter of appellatives may be used in the same way, both in the singular and plural,
thus, in a late example; we had இருளிறருஇ which is the same with இரு
ணட்தனி : so for the plural; பலஇறத்தனவாயமல்லெ *flowers variegated*
with many colours.

I shall conclude this Section by adducing as an example, a Ven'bâ,
in which the third person neuter singular of the appellative is used
throughout :

வெநஇறடெறசெமபொானவிநிகடறடெவைமுததம
பொறஇபிறறுமபுமுகைததேட்டதனினி   மெ
கறஇபிடெற
பெணணைமுகுகல்லறதத்தேடபொாபபொருளினபம
ஙைணணமுகுசெயதமையதடெகா   ன்

Here the appellative பொறிஇற்றும் is used for the verbal of the
preterite, and the others, as verbs, in the third person neuter singular.
The sense is the same as if the author had written, வெறியினதாகுஞ்
செம்பொன் &c. The meaning is: *Gold is in the mountain, pearls are in
the sea, and the sweetness of the honey lies in the beauteous flower buds :
so chastity is the beauty of a woman, durable riches are found in virtue,
and benevolence is the embellishment of the eye.*

I have dwelt the more at length on appellatives, because in them,
principally, consist the peculiar character and difficulty of the syntax in
this dialect.

SECTION THE THIRD.
OF NOUNS ADJECTIVE.

XVI. In the other grammar we stated, that adjectives, as சில *few*,
பல *many* &c. are called உரிச்சொல். But of words expressing mode,
which are all comprehended by the Tamils under this general term,
many in this dialect, are joined, not only as adjectives to nouns, but also
as adverbs to verbs: thus, நனி,தவ,சால,உறு,கழி, கூர், all which are terms
of increment, are joined with nouns; as, நனிதவதடோதான *an austere penitent,* உறுதுணை *effectual succour ;* or with verbs; as, நனிசடோனனுனை *he
spoke much,* சாலடோதணட்டான *he received abundantly :* thus, in the
Rámáyan am of Camben, we have

கலஇமபுலஇஙககணடுருகபடெணைகனிநினறுன
where the word நனி is used adverbially, and signifies sweetly; the meaning
being : *The maid stood, looking so sweetly, that the very herbage and
rocks would have melted, had they beheld her :* so in another poet, the
word கழி, which has various significations, is used in the same line both
as an adjective and an adverb.

கழிதுவணபடதழிமா - - - நி
கழிவிட விணைவின்மாயநதார்

*He swiftly discharging a shower of sharp pointed arrows, they suddenly
perished.* Here கழிதுவணை signifies a *sharp point,* and கழிவிட *to
discharge swiftly.* All words of this kind will be found in the dictionary.

XVII. Adjectives are frequently formed from substantives. On this subject, I shall here add a few remarks to those contained in the other grammar.

First: the oblique of the noun is often used as an adjective; thus, கடாப்புளினமார்பு *a breast adorned with a glittering chain.* This is also done in prose: thus, in the work entitled Silappadigáram, we have மணவாயதெதனற்ல *the fragrant southern breeze,* நிழதி ற்சோலை *a shady grove:* and in the same work போராசிறுயபிறபுகார்கராத்துகொளாவலன *Cóvalan a native of the city Pucàr of perpetual celebrity:* where போராச றிபயின, and நகாத்து are used as adjectives.

Secondly: nouns substantive ending in மை express quality in the abstract: as, கருமை *blackness;* வெண்மை *whiteness;* அருமை *difficulty.* From such nouns, when the மை is preceded by உ, adjectives are formed in the following ways.—By simply dropping இ; so from அருமை, அரும பொருள *a difficult thing;* from பசமை, பசங்கிளி *a green parrot.*—By dropping மை; so from சிறுமை, சிறுபொருள *a small thing.*—Or the மை being dropped the உ suffers elision, and இய is substituted: as, அறி யபொருள, பசியகிளி, சிறியபொருள,—Or dropping the மை, the conso- nant which preceded it, if a rough letter, is doubled: this method is used only when the following noun begins with a vowel which causes elision of the உ: thus from பசமை, பசிஇலை *a green leaf;* from நெடுமை, நெ டடெழுத்து *a long letter;* from குறுமை, குறடெழுத்து *a short letter.*— Or without doubling the consonant, the first syllable if short is made long, but the உ always suffers elision if followed by a vowel: thus, பச மை, (1) பாசிஇல *a green leaf;* கருமை, காடெலி *a black rat;* பெருமை, பேடொலி *a great sound.* But if the உ which preceded மை be annexed to one of the final consonants, the உ is dropped: thus, from பெருமை and நலம we form பேர்நலம.

---

(1) It appears from Nannùl, that the word பசமை may also become an adjective, before words beginning with க,ச,த,ப, by dropping மை, changing the second syllable to the nasal corresponding to each of those letters, and the அ of the first syllable to இ: thus, பைஙங்கிளி, பைஞருசோல், பையாந்தார், பைம்மெபொன.

These methods, however, cannot be indiscriminately used with all the nouns of which we are speaking; some may become adjectives in all these ways, others, in some only: thus, from இறுமை we have இறிடி, இறறடி, இறுஎமை, இற்யகமை; from பசுமை, பாசில், பசிசில், பசமஇசி, பஇயஇசி; from கருமை, காரஇசி, கருமஇவண, கரியமுகம; of all the above appellatives the first syllable may be lengthened. But from அருமை, we have அருடிபொருள், அரியபொருள், and not அிகாரிஇல; from புதமை, we have புதககமை, புதியகமை, or doubling the rough ச, புததிசி, not புததிசி; from கெதஇமை, கெநுகஇதறு, கெஇயஇதறு: of all these we cannot lengthen the first syllable. From குறுமை we have only குஇககஇதறு; கொஇமை, again, cannot double the rough ட, but may only be formed as in கொடுகஇகால், கொஇயமஇஉம.

On this subject, Pavananti himself tells us, in his Nannül, that no rules can be given, but that we must observe the practice of ancient writers. I thought it right, however, to say thus much, in order that the student may know the etymology as well as the meaning, of such words. Information of this kind cannot be obtained from the dictionary, since these adjectives are never written separately, but are always joined to some noun which they qualify.

Thirdly: nouns ending in மை not preceded by உ, but either by இ, இ, i, or ம், become adjectives by dropping மை, and taking ய: thus, from உடைமை possession is formed உடைய, from இனிமை sweetness, இனிய; from இமை badness, இய; from கொஇமை tenderness, கொய்ய. After these words, a rough consonant following is never doubled: thus உடையபொருள், இனியசொல், இயதம, கொய்யமலர். Many nouns which do not end in மை, but in இ annexed to some other consonant, add ய, as before, but undergo no elision: thus, from மலை hill comes மலைய; from வளை bracelet, வளைய; from கனஇ bud, கனைய; from கை hand, கைய, Thus, in the poem Chintamani we have:

கவஇயஇலமுருசனாவியுருமுமலர்
கவஇயநாகமுகஇகொஇகமுகாதினைர்ச
இவஇயஇசனபகமஇஉஇகஇயாஇஇடறஇ
முஇஇவளாஇமறதுஇமுஇஇதஇகஇதாஇஇஉ
இஇகமாஇஇயஇஇஇயபகம-இஉகவி.

Presenting the Nílam from the water springs, and the Súlli and the Nágam overspread with flower buds, the Cóngam, the Shen'bagam whose branches are covered with scented flowers, and the Véngei, he sung all the praises of the chief of deities.

The poet here enumerates various kinds of flowers which Sívagan offers to his god, whilst repeating his praises. The word சுஷ்ண means a spring in the mountains; ய being added it becomes an adjective, qualifying the noun சீலை, and implying, that this flower grows in the water : கஷ்ண is *a flower* not yet blown; and ய being added, the sentence imports that the tree called Nágam was covered with buds : இணர் signifies *a flower*, கிஷ்ண *a branch*; and ய being added to the latter, the meaning of இணர்செவ்வயேசென்பகம is, *the flowery branched Shen'bagam.* Here இணர் is used in the oblique, and consequently doubles the following rough consonant ; it is employed as an adjective, *flowery*, in the manner already explained : நறுமை signifies *an agreeable scent*, and becomes an adjective in நறிஞர் *a fragrant flower*, according to a late rule.

Fourthly : words ending in மை preceded by any vowel except உ may drop the மை and be joined without any other change to the noun which they qualify : after these words, however, a following rough letter is doubled: thus, from தனிமை *unconnectedness*, we have தனிசேசால் an *unconnected word* ; from உரிமை *property*, உரிசேசால் *a word of property*, i. e. *adjective* ; from உடைமை *possession*, உடைபொருள *things possessed.* Words, however, in which the vowel before மை is அ, become adjectives by dropping ஐ only : thus, from இளமை *youth*, இளமபயிர் *young corn* ; from பழமை *antiquity*, பழமபகை *inveterate hatred.*

Sometimes the ம too is dropped, as இளயது *youth;* and sometime the அ which remains, is changed to இய, as in இளயயது, பழயபடி.

Fifthly : nouns ending in மை preceded by a consonant become adjectives by simply dropping the மை : thus, from வெண்மை *whiteness*, we have ஓணாகுருகு *while heron*, ஓணாசிலை *a while stone*; from ஒணமை *splendour*, ஓணபொருள *a splendid thing*; from ஒயமை *heat*, ஒயபகை *fiery hatred*, ஒருசரம *a fiery-arrow*; from ஒசமை which among other significations, means *perfection* in any thing, come ஒசிநெல, *ripe paddy*; ஒசந்தமிழ *the perfect or pure Tamil language*, ஒசம்பொன *pure gold*. We have already said that words which have ய before மை become adjectives by dropping the மை and taking another ய: thus, from ஒசய்மை *redness*, is formed ஒசய்யகுருதி *red blood*; such words may, however, follow the present rule; and we may say ஒசங்குருதி &c.

It has been stated, that the neuter singular of all appellatives may end in அது. If this termination அது be dropped, the remainder serves as an adjective in every gender: thus, from the appellative இறந்தது we have இறந்தகை *a strong hand*; from விளைவினது, விளைவினதேர் *a swift chariot*.

Certain adjectives, of the formation of which we have already spoken, may come also under this rule: thus, ஒகாடிய may be referred to ஒகாடியது; கரிய to கரியது; ஒவயய to ஒவயயது; உடைடய to உடைடயது &c.

Lastly: the nominative form is frequently employed, in this dialect, as an adjective, in every case except the vocative: thus, பூணமார்பன for பூசாயதமார்பன, கற்று for கல்லாலயற்று, சாததணமகன for சாததற குடகன, மஷயருவி for மஷயினற்றருவி, மஷசசாரல for மஷயினது சாரல, மஷகருகை for மஷகடகுகை.

This style of expression will appear, at first, somewhat difficult and obscure; but when practice and observation shall have rendered it familiar, it will not only be understood from the context, but its conciseness will be found elegant and pleasing.

SECTION THE FOURTH.

OF PRONOUNS.

XVIII. As pronouns in Latin Grammar are divided into primitives, derivatives, demonstratives, relatives and possessives, I shall treat of them according to this arrangement.

First: The primitive pronouns in this dialect are, நான், யான் *I*; நீ *thou*; நாம், யாம், நாங்கள், யாங்கள் *we*; நீர், நீயிர், நீவிர் *ye*; எல்லீர் *all ye*. They are inflected with the terminations common to other nouns. (See Chap. II. Sec. 1.) In order, therefore, to decline any one of them, it is sufficient to know its oblique, or the intermediate change which takes place in passing from the nominative to the other cases. The oblique of நான் and யான், is என்; which, with the addition of the casual terminations, gives எனவன, எனளுல், எறகு, or எனக்கு, எனவின், என்று, எனக்கண. The oblique forms of நீ, are, உன், நின், நுன: it is, therefore, declined, உனவன, or நினவன, or நுனவன; உனளுல், or நினளுல், or நுன்ளுல், உனக்கு or நுனக்கு; நிறகு (1) or நினக்கு; &c. The oblique forms of the first person plural are, எம், நம், எக்கள, நங்கள. These give எமமைம, நமமைம; எங்கள்ன, நங்கள்ன; எமமான், நமமான்; எங்க

---

(1) This form is disallowed in the Grammars and even by Beschi himself in his Tonnúl Vilácam, for though it be a rule that

எம்காணறம்காணுண்கஜாருபிறகு

ஒதால்-புஷ-உக-ரூத.

In the fourth case என், *(the termination of the oblique) is changed to* ற்.

Yet by another special rule, the application of the foregoing to நின is expressly forbidden : thus in Nannúl

தனௌனௌனபவறநீ றுறுஞவன்ணையௌயா

ஏறுழுன்னிஞ் றியலபாமுற   ஏவ

நன்-ஒமய-லிறி-ரூத.

The final என் *of the words* தன் *and* என், *are changed into the rough letter* ற; *but the final of* நின் *is retained.*

Nevertheless, examples of நிற்கு are found in Chintáman'i and other poems; and therefore it has been admitted in the present Grammar by Beschi, who following the old poets, has used this form in his Témbávan'i.

னால, நடுகனால; எமகது, நமகது; எங்கட்கு, நடுகட்கு; or எங்களுககு, நடுகளுககு; &c. The oblique forms of the second person plural are, உம, நும, உடுகள. These give உமமை, நுமமை, உடுகளை.

Observe that the double consonant in the middle of the foregoing and following pronouns may be written single: thus, for எனவை, எமமை, நமமை, தனவை, தமமை &c. we may write எவை, எமை, நமை, தவை, தமை. Observe, also, that the distinction which is made in common Tamil between நாம and நாடுகள, is not preserved in this dialect. In fact, நாடுகள, நீடுகள, அவர்கள, with their cases, are hardly ever used.

It has been stated, that the oblique of a noun may be substituted for any of its cases. It is the same with pronouns: thus, in Chintamani, we have எனனைலறபொறுதுபபர்யாடு for எனவையலலால, *who, except me, would forgive?* So, in the same work, எறகாணவந்தீர் for எனவைக காணவந்தீர் *you came to see me.* Such instances, however, are rare.

XIX. Secondly: Derivative pronouns answering to the Latin *nostras (belonging to our sect or country), vestras, (belonging to your sect or country),* are formed, in this dialect, from the oblique plural of the primitive: thus, from நம, எம, are formed நமன, எமன, நமன, எமன, நமர், எமர், *nostras, nostrates, a person, or persons, belonging to our sect or country;* from உம, நும, are formed உமன, நுமன, உமன, நுமன, உமர், நுமர், *vestras, vestrates, a person, or persons, belonging to your sect or country:* from தம, the oblique of the pronoun தாம, (in like manner,) are derived தமன, தமன, தமர். All these are inflected by simply adding the casual terminations: thus, நமவை, நமவின், நமனா, நடுகுல, நமனால, நமரால, &c. and so of the rest. These pronouns are seldom inflected, except in the plural, when they frequently mean *my, your, his, her, relations,* &c. Thus, in the poem Negizhdam by king Adiviran, we read :

உாவுதீர்ககளுடுகடஇடுததமாவில   த
தருருடனிமவைமயிலலிததததானபொருவ
மருவியமநுமையிலவபழடுகருபானவையயா
லிாவலர்தமரிணுயினியாராவ   டுா
    லுக நவைனறுதுசெனறபடலம-உலு-கவி.

Since the well earned riches which we bountifully distribute in this world girt with the blue ocean, have the power of acquiring for us reward in the life on which we shall hereafter enter, the poor should be dearer to us than our own relations. Here relations is expressed by தமர். So, in Chintamani we have கோனறமர், *the king's relations.*

XX. Thirdly: The demonstrative pronouns in this dialect, are, இவன் *this man;* இவள் *this woman;* இது, or இதன் *this thing;* இவர் *these men,* or *women;* இவை *these things;* அவன் *that man;* அவள், *that woman;* அது, or அதன் *that thing;* அவர் *those men,* or *women;* அவை *those things;* and உவன், உவள், உது, உவர், உவை, which point to intermediate objects: thus, இவன், is he who is near; அவன், he who is distant; உவன், he who is between both.

Of these pronouns, those which are masculine and feminine are declined like the derivatives: thus, இவனை, அவனை, உவனை, &c. as are also the neuters, இதன், அதன். These last scarcely ever take இத ற்கு, அதற்கு, for their datives, which are almost always இதற்கு, அதற்கு; although இவன் &c. take இவற்கு, and இவற்கு &c. indifferently. The neuters இது, அது, உது, are declined thus: இதை, or இததை; இததால், or இதினால்; இதற்கு; இதினின்று, இதின், or இதினின; இதினாகண்; so also அது, உது. Their plurals இவை, அவை, உவை form the oblique by changing ஐ into அற்று: as, இவற்று, அவற்று, உவற்று. These, again, may take the termination இன்; as இவற்றின், &c. and by adding the casual terminations to either form, we have இவற்றை, or இவற்றினை; இவற்றுல்; இவற்றுக்கு, or இவற்றிற்கு; இவற்றின், or இவற்றினின், இவற்றினது; இவற்றினகண். So likewise with the other two.

There is one more demonstrative pronoun, தான் *himself, herself, itself;* plural தாம், or தாங்கள். Each of these forms its oblique by changing ஆ into அ, as தன், தம், தங்கள்; to which, as with the primitives, the signs of the cases are added: thus, தனவை, தமமை, தங்கள், &c.

XXI. Fourthly: In Tamil, there is no relative pronoun answering to *who, which;* but it's place is supplied in the manner explained in the

other grammar, No. 124. There are, however, the corresponding inter-
rogatives, *who? what?* viz. for the singular masculine, எவன, யாவன;
for the singular feminine, எவள, யாவள; for both genders and numbers,
ஆர், யார், யாரை; for both genders in the plural only, எவர், யாவர்.
These are all declined like இவன, இவள, இவர், &c. For the neuter
singular எது, யாது, யாவது; for the neuter plural எவை, யாவை. These
are declined like இது, இவை, &c. Hence come the words எவரும, யா
ரும், யாவரும், *all persons;* எவையும், யாவையும், *all things.*

The word எவன, besides being used for the masculine of the interro-
gative *who?* serves also for the neuter of both numbers: as, எவனது
what is that? எவனவை *what are those,* &c.

இறைகாகருஙகாபஇபவன செயயுமகவர்
றைறைகாகருஙகாபஇபத   எவ
திருவ - கூ, அஇ - ா, குற.

*What avails the caution of imprisonment; the chief security of woman
is her virtue.* Here, *what avails it,* is rendered by எவன செயயும. The
word என is used in the same way; whence the expression எனரும *what
will happen? what will ensue?* Thus, again, Tiruvall'uver:

ஒதி தததககாஒனனரும்முவர்.

What though the Sea roar? i. e. it will not, on that account, pass its
bounds. In the same sense is also used எனன, or more commonly in this
dialect எனென. This may likewise be rendered *wherefore?* as, எனவன
யாஒவில் *if you ask, wherefore.*

Observe, finally, that for யாது, *what,* we may, by apocope, write
யா; and that this is joined, not only with nouns, as, யாடஒபாருன,
யாகருஇன, (in the same way as we say எடஒபாருன, எகருஇன, of
which I shall presently speak); but also to verbs, as, யாசஒசெயதாய *what
hast thou done?* Example:

யாகாயாாாயி இநாகாககதாவாககா ற
சொகாப்பர்சொஇடுகருபபட இ
திருவ - ்ஈ, அஇ - ா, குற.

*Though you guard nothing else, guard your tongue; for ruin will ensue
from licentious speech.*

XXII. Fifthly: The Tamils have no possessive pronoun; for, although எனது, நமது &c. are aptly rendered by the possessive pronouns *my, mine; thy, thine;* they are, in fact, either the genitive cases of எனை, நம, &c. as we have already seen; or they are compounds of the obliques என, நம, &c. with அது, and have the force of, *this belongs to me, to us,* &c. considered in either way, they may be used by themselves without a governing noun; and thus, to the question, *whose is this?* may be answered, எனது *it is mine.*

Besides the pronouns already specified, the Tamils have others, which may be termed pronouns adjective, and of which we have spoken in No. 48 of the other grammar. These are இந்த-இனை, or simply இ *this,* அந்த-அனை or அ *that,* எந்த-எனை or எ *which?*

இ,அ,எ. They differ from the pronouns of which we have hitherto treated, for they have neither case, gender, nor number; but are used as adjectives, which, in this language, must always be joined to substantives: as, இந்தஅ, இஅனஅ, இஅ. Respecting these pronouns, P have one remark to add to what I have said in the other grammar. The adjective letters இ, அ, எ, may be joined not only with all nouns, but also with participles: for, these, although they are formed from verbs, are termed பெயரெச்சம், *defective nouns:* thus, இசெசான்னஅவுனர்ச்சி *this instruction which is imparted;* அத்தகெதபொருள் *that thing which is given;* எசெசெயதகருமம *what work that is performed?* Nouns appellative, formed from substantives, even when conjugated as verbs, as already explained, may also take these letters: thus, இநநூலெலயபெய நெது *what is the name of this science;* இமமாடஅவெறபிறஅது *these bullocks are of that mountain;* நானிஅஊரிடேஎன *I am of this village.*

XXIII. Finally, observe that, in this dialect, no use is made, either in the pronouns or the verbs, of that mode of expression according to which, in common Tamil, we employ நீர் and அவர் as honorifics for *thou* and *he;* for, even in commentaries, I have rarely seen எனறுர், சொனனுர், &c. as honorifics for எனறுன, சொனனுன, &c.; and in the poets themselves, this figure is hardly ever found. The only instance which I have met with, is in the poem Chintàman´i, where it is used to express an overflow of love and joy; the story connected with it, is as follows : The queen Vijeiyei, whilst pregnant of her first child, was forced to flee from an insurrection in which the king was assassinated by his prime minister: in her flight she was delivered of her son Sivagan, in a place appropriated to the burning of the dead, a spot considered particularly ill-omened and unclean. Here the child was found by a merchant, who, being ignorant of his parentage, took him away, with the design of bringing him up as his own. In the mean time, the queen retired to the desert, and spent her days in penance. At length the boy, arrived at manhood, having learned the particulars of his birth, and the place of his mother's abode, goes thither: the mother is delighted on again beholding her son, whom she now finds of ripened years, and renowned for his military exploits; and in a transport of joy and affection, immediately accosts him thus, சிவகசாட்டிேேர். I shall give the whole stanza, as it exemplifies many of the foregoing remarks :

வாட்டிற்றுக்குருசிறனவெணவாளமாகதத்தீததுக
காட்டகதத்துமைமசீததகயதஇெயற்காணவந்தீ ர்
செட்டிையைபருஇமார்பிறச்சதசாயிப் ேோ
பூடடாங்குணடெசநதாமணையடிேநாவேவனருள.
விபகியாரிலமபகம-உய ரு - கவி.

The mother, addressing her son, uses the words சாயிப்ேர், உமைம, வந்தீர்; in all which, the plural is put honorifically for the singular.—வாட்டிற்றற்குருசிறனவெண, here, குருசில் means *king*, and திறல் *bravery* is used adjectively, by rule XVII. 2d. signifies *brave;* வாள means *sword*, but, by rule XVII is taken as an adjective, and the sense is the same as வாளாஎவ்யதிறல்: by rule VI. 5, ள is changed into ட, த into ட, and ல into ற, வாட்டிற்றற்குருசில்; and by the same rule, since குருசில் is the accusative, the ல is changed to ற, and the following த to ற; and one of these being dropped, we have குருசிறனவெணவாளமாகதத்றசீதது. Here, as before, வாள has the force of வாளாஎல்யவமர்; அமர் signifies *battle;* அமாகதத்று is the seventh case, கண, in treating of which, IX. 7. we stated, that for கண other nouns may be used which denote place; அகப is a noun of this kind, and, since it ends in ம, its oblique is formed in தத, according to the rules on that head; சீதது, *by quitting.* காட்டகதத்துமைமசீதத, here காடு, the genus being put for the species.

signifies the same as சுடுகாடு *a place for burning the dead,* காடு is it's oblique, by rule VII. 4. and காட்டகத்து is the seventh case, as above; சீத்த, a participle preterite.—கயத்தியெறகாணவந்தீர், கயத்தி is an appellative feminine, from கயம், by rule XII. 3. and signifies *ill-omened* ; எறகாணவந்தீர், for எனவிஷகாணவந்தீர், என being used for எள வள, by rule XVIII. and changed to எற், by rule VI. 4.—செட்டிஎ மயருதிமார்பிறசிஉக, செடு means *beauty,* and, by rule XVII, its oblique செட்டு, is used as an adjective, *beautiful* ; இளம், an adjective, from இளமை, by rule XVII. 4. இளைபருதி; *the sun newly risen,* which shines without scorching, to which the poet wishing to compare the youth's breast, instead of saying பருதியைபபொதியமார்பு, uses the word adjectively, by rule XVII, and writes பருதிமார்பு. This mode of expression may be referred to the metaphor, which is termed by the Tamils உருவகம், and is very common in this language; மார்பிற is put for மார்பி எ, on account of the following ச, see rule VI. 4. and is the oblique of மார்பு, by rule VIII. 1st; it has here the force of the fourth case, by VIII. 4.—சிவகசாமீயிஉோ, the vocative plural, by rule IX. 8.—உளட்ட ரகருணடசெதகாமணையடிஉோஉ, உோஉ is put for உோக, as will be explained hereafter; தாமணையடி is a metaphor, as before, and is the same with தாமணையபபொதியமடி. the poet praises the flower தாமரை for its colour, saying, that it has obtained the red hue which is infused into it, by drinking அாககு; in expressing this, he uses the word உளட்டு, which is put for உளட்டும், the participle future of the verb உளட்டுதல் *to infuse;* and this, again, is used instead of the participle preterite, உளட்டின், all which is accounted for in the rule which follows: lastly, செம், which, on account of the following த, becomes செந், is an adjective, from the noun செமமை, by rule XVII. 5. The meaning of the stanza is :

You are come, O Lord Sivagen, whose breast (beams with mild splendor) *like the rising sun, to visit me ill omened,* (wretch), *who quilted in the field of battle the king* (thy father,) *valiant in war, and abandoned you in the burning place of the dead,* (you are come) *paining your feet, which are as the red Tàmarei imbued with the* (rich) *colour of the lac that it has sucked up.*

I was induced to parse this stanza thus minutely, because it affords no less than four and twenty examples of the foregoing rules.

APPENDIX.

XXIV. I shall here offer some observations, to complete the chapter on nouns·

It was stated, (XII. 3d,) that many nouns of two short syllables, and ending in ம, may also terminate in ன; as அறன், மனன், குணன் : but that the rule is not general, and that we ought to follow the practice of ancient writers. I have now to observe:

First: Many nouns ending in ம், and consisting of two syllables, of which the first is long, frequently change the final அ ம into உ; as, for யோகம், யோகு : but I have never seen an instance of this, except when there followed a word beginning with a vowel, by which the உ was cut off: thus, in a verse of which I shall speak hereafter we find the word எமாற்றல ; where எகு is used for எமம custody, and the உ is cut off by the following அ of the verb ஆற்றல to do. Hence, எமாற்றல is rendered to guard. A certain author uses சீதுணட for சீல்குணட ;and, in the same way, காகுற்று is put for காமகுற்று. Some polysyllables, even though short, follow this rule, either with, or without the elision of the final உ. Thus, Tiruvalluven has நடுகக்றறகாடடியவர், for நடுகமற றகாடடியவர் the man of knowledge is without wavering : thus, also, உலகு for உலகம. But here, also, we must be guided by the practice of the ancients.

Second: It has been stated, that இது, அது, may become இதன அதன. I have here to add that verbals in து follow the same rule; thus, வருகி னறது or வருகினறதன ; வநதது or வநததன ; வருவது or வருவதன : also ஆவது or ஆவதன: and for யாவது, யாவதன ; and for யாது, யாதன. All these words are declined like இவன ; so that we frequently see ஆவதறகு, வருவதறகு, வநததறகு, &c. used as datives.

Third: We stated, in the other grammar, that nouns of number are declined through all the cases, and that all numerals below a thousand end in உ; these may also end in அன: thus ஓனறன, இரணடன, மூனறன, நான கன, ஐநதன, ஆறன, எழுன, எடடன, ஒனபதன, இருபதன, முபபதன, &c.

I have not, however, seen (*) பத்து, and தூறு, varied in this way: these words, when they terminate in ன், are inflected like இவன், and may then be used as adjectives (ordinals) ; so that ஆறன், எழன், &c. mean either *six*, *seven*, &c. or the *sixth*, the *seventh*, &c. Thus, in Nannûl, we have ஆறனுருபு, எழனுருபு, for ஆறுருபு, எழுருபு.

CHAPTER III.

OF THE VERB.

XXV. Verbs, which are termed வினை, are not denoted in this, as in the common dialect, by the verbal in இறது, but by the verbal in ல்; as, செயயல் *doing or to do*, படித்தல் *reading or to read:* under this form, they are given in the dictionary. Those which, in common Tamil, end in இறது, in this dialect terminate generally in தல்; and those which end in கிறது, in ததல்: thus, பணிதல் *to worship;* அறிதல் *to know;* உணர்தல் *to understand;* அடித்தல் *to beat;* படித்தல் *to read, learn;* படைத்தல் *to create.* Some ending in இறது terminate in ல், without the த: as செயயல் *to do;* பெயயல் *to rain;* அணியல் *to adorn;* பணியல் *to submit.* Those, however, which have உ before இறது, usually change the உ into அ, and add ல்; as, தடவல் *to stroke or rub;* உதவல் *to assist;* சொல்லல் *to say,* கொளளல் *to buy.* Nevertheless, they may terminate according to the general rule: as, தடவுதல், உதவுதல், சொல்லுதல்.

XXVI. We stated, in the other grammar, that many verbs which, properly, end in க்கிறது, are made, by syncope, to terminate in க்கிறது; when, according to the general rule there laid down, they form their pre-

---

(*) It is singular that Beschi should not recollect having met with these words used with the termination அன், since, though not common, they occur in works on grammar, with which he must have been acquainted : for instance.

ஒன்றுமுதலொன்பானிறுதிமுனைஏர்
தினைநபத்தேறறுகடெவாயதம

      தொல். குறியியலகாபயுணியல—௬௩, சூ.

நாறுயிரமுனவருடுங்காஎவ்
தறனியறகைழுதல் எக்கினைவி:

      தொல். குறியியலகாபயுணியல—சூ௭, சூ௫.

terite in கி்டேனை : of this kind are, அடக்கிறது *to refrain;* முடுக்கிறது *to urge.* But since these verbs ought properly to end in கு்கிறது, in this dialect, according to the rule just laid down, they drop இறது, change the உ into அ, and take ல், so that they become அடக்கல், முடுக்கல்; are also அடக்குசல், முடுக்குதல்: this removes all doubt respecting the formation of the preterite; if, for example, the verb be தீதல் *to renounce,* the preterite must be தீதேதன; if தீக்கல் *to avoid,* தீகிடேனை.

XXVII. The verbal of which we have been speaking is constantly and elegantly used in this dialect.

First: It is used as a noun, and inflected with all the cases: thus, போதல்லைவிலைகி்குனை *he prevented the going;* சொல்லாலறிந்தேன *I apprehended through the medium of speech;* கொடைகின்தவில்லிது *giving is more delightful than receiving;* உணாதற்கடிபுகழ் *knowledge is the object of praise.*

Secondly: It is sometimes used absolutely: as, அறிதற்பொருட்டு *for the sake of knowing;* போதற்காரணமாக *on account of going.* For instance, a person observes something moving, and doubts whether it be an ox or a man; at length, he perceives some signs by which he knows that it is a man. I say of him மகனுதனுணிந்தால *he ascertained it to be a man,* that is, மகனுயிருக்கிறுனென்றுதுணிந்தான.

Third: It is often used for the infinitive: as, செய்யலேவணடும *it is necessary to do;* போதல்லைவிலைக்கி்குனை *he prevented going;* பாடஇலுனானகதான் *he learned to sing.*

<hr/>

SECTION THE FIRST.
OF THE INDICATIVE.

XXVIII. Of the five moods, this language wants the optative and subjunctive; and of the five tenses, the imperfect and the preter-pluperfect. These deficiencies are supplied in the manner described in the grammar of the common dialect. I proceed to treat of the indicative.

XXIX. In conjugating the verbs, the same terminations serve for the present, the preterite, and, with certain exceptions, for the future; this last tense having, in this dialect, some that are peculiar to itself, of which I shall speak in the proper place.

The terminations common to all are :

For the first person singular, என், எ : as, நடந்தேன், நடந்தேனெ, *I walked.*

For the second person singular, ஆய், ஐ, இ : as, நடந்தாய், நடந்தஎன், நடந்தி, *thou walkedst.*

For the third person singular masculine, ஆன், அன : as நடந்தான்; நட ந்தஎன; feminine, ஆள, அஎ : as நடந்தாள, நடந்தஎள; neuter து. as நட ந்தது *it walked;* or in the preterite, it has ற்று, when preceded by இ: as, சொல்லினது or சொல்லிற்று; ஆயினது, ஆயிற்று, போயினது, போ யிற்று; in the future, the termination of the third person neuter singular is உம் ; as, நடக்கும்.

For the first person plural, ஆம், அம், எம், எம, ஓம் : as, நடந்தாம் நடந்தஎம், நடந்தோ்ம், நடந்தேனெம், நடந்தோாம், *we walked.*

For the second person plural, ஈர், இர : as நடந்தீர், நடந்தீர, நடந் தனிர, *you walked.*

For the third person masculine, and feminine, ஆர், அர : as, நடந்தா ர், நடந்தஎர் *they walked;* for the neuter, அ : as, நடந்தன, or simply நடந்த : thus, in the poem Negizhdam at the close of a stanza, the author, speaking of the clouds, says, உருகொொடுட்டஎட *having acquired a form and returned,* for மீணடன; and in another stanza : போனஎ னருண நின்றமெலவனதொொடஎடபொான்ஒென்பபொாழிந்த *the clouds in libe-rality like him* (the king) *poured down* (rain abundantly), for பொாழிந்த ன. In like manner for (*) சொரிவனபொால we find சொரிவபொால், for செயதன்வாதலில், செய்தவாதவில்; for (‡) மிகஎனவாஇ, மிகக்வாஇ. Some-times, though rarely, கஎ is added in the plural; not only in the second and third persons, as நடந்தீர்கள், நடந்தார்கா *they walked;* but also in the first, as நடந்தஎமகள், நடந்தஎமகள், நடப்பெவகள், நடப்பனஎவஎள.

XXX. First: The present tense, called நிகழ்காலம, is formed either, as in the common dialect, in இடேறன, which mode is hardly ever used ;

(*) சொரிதல் to pour.

(‡) மீருதல் to abound.

or in இனறேன: or by adding தினறேன to the negative form. (†) The sense of the compound is, however, positive; and this is accounted for by the use of the negative form for the positive gerund: as, for நடவா, செய்யா, for நடந்து, செய்து; which will be explained in the proper place. The present tense, then, may have any of the following forms: நடகிறேன, நடகினறேன, நடவாகினறேன, நடகினறனென, நடவாகினற னென, &c. To conjugate these forms, it is only necessary to add the abovementioned terminations, for the several persons.

XXXI. Secondly: With respect to the preterite, I have nothing to add to what is contained in the other grammar; so that, to the following preterites, நடந்தேன, படித்ததேன, நீகினேன, செயதேன, &c. we have only to affix the terminations abovementioned. I have, however, seen, in old authors of repute, several preterites for which I can find no rule. Such are the following: திநிஇனென for திறுத்திஞன he caused to stop, (v. a.) தழீஇஞன for தழுவிஞன he embraced, கழீஇஞன for கழுவிஞன he washed, விழீஇஞன for விழுந்தான he fell, வெரீஇஞன for வெருவி ஞன he feared, இரீஇஞன for இருந்தான he was, எழீஇஞன for எழுந தான he arose. From these instances, I think we may deduce this general rule: all verbs, of which the preterites end in உவிஞன or உந்தன, may drop this termination, and, taking ஈ, have, by அவைபெடை, ஈஇ னென: thus, கழுவிஞனென, கழீஇனென, &c. இருந்தேன, இரீஇனென, &c. From these words, you will often find திநிஇ, கழீஇ, &c. for the gerund; and for the participle preterite, by adding ய to the gerund, திநிஇய, தழீஇய, கழீஇய, &c. I have also met with கொளீஇ and கொடீஇ, for

---

(†) According to the Tamil grammarians the termination is அதினறேன; so that it does not appear necessary to account for this formation, by supposing, with Beschi, that தினறேன is added to the negative form.

அதினறுகினறுகிதிறுழுவிடததி

வணமபாள்கழுபொழுததைறவிவண்யிடைகிவன.

அதினறு - இன்று, & திறு are the characterisick syllables of the present tense of the verb in the three places (persons) & five Pàlàs (2 numbers and 3 genders.)

நன - பதவியல் - ய்ஈ, ஒஈ.

சொஉறு ; வஹாஇ for வஹாததது ; செஇ for சொர்உது, செஇ for செஇ, and that for செர்உ.து. Example :

சல்தைதாற்பொருளசெய்தைதைமாற்றலபசுமட்
கலைதைதுண்ரிபெயஇரீஇயம்
து

திருவ - சூலஈஈ, அஇ - ஃ, குற.

Here, பெய்இரீஇயறஉ is put for பெய்இருஉதஇற்று. The meaning is : *To guard with anxiety ill-gotten wealth, is like trying to keep water in an unbaked earthen vessel.* Another author has :

வெரிஇயபுட்குலஉஉமஇழுக்துவிமயின்

The flock of birds frightened rose up and screamed.

XXXII. Thirdly: The future is formed according to the rules laid down in the other grammar. Those verbs, however, which I have there stated to have their future in வென், may, in this dialect, form it also in குவென், thus, செயகுவென from செய்தைல to do, அணிகுவென from அணிதைல *to adorn*. Besides the common terminations for the first person, என், என் ; as, செய்வென, செய்குவென ; கடபடென, கடபடென ; this tense has likewise அஃல் and அன் : as கடப்பல, கடப்பன ; காண்டஃல், காண்டன் ; &c. It also terminates in உ : as, வாஉஉது, கூஉஉது, சொல்இஉது, வருஉது, for வாஉழென, கூஉறுென, சொஉல்இவென, வருவென ; and உண்கு, செய்கு, செஉறு, for உண்டபென, செய்உவென, செஉல்இஉவென. By adding ம் to these, we get the first person plural : as, வாஉழதுமஉ, கூஉறுதுமஉ, உண குஉமஉ, செய்குஉமஉ. Thus, in the opening stanza of Chintàman'i, we have தெவாஉஇதெவன்வனசெய்அடிசோதுமன்தெஉ், *we will approach the rosy feet of the God of gods*, for சொஉவாமஉ. The other persons take only the common terminations. அ being that of the third person neuter plural, we have கடபபல் ; இஇரிஅன் ; செய்அன், or செய்குவன் ; மஃலர்வன ; நீகஉகுவன்.

The second person of the imperative, with the addition of ப or மார், serves for the third person masculine plural of the future : thus, எைப, எனமார் ; கடப்ப, க—மார் ; கெட்ப, கேண்மார் ; மொஃழிப, மொஃழிமார் : accordingly we find எைப்பஃலோ, மொஃழிப்புஉவர், for எைபார், மொஃழி வார்.

Sometimes மஉழுர் is used with the same force as மார் : as, எனமஉழுர் for எனமார், மொஉஃழிஉமஉழுர், for மொஃழிஉவார். The ancient and celebrated author Tolcáppianár, in his grammatical writings, frequently uses this form : as எனமறுர்புலவர், மொழிமறுர்புலவர். Sometimes, too, the short syllable மர் is put for மார் : as, எனமர், மொழிமர். Example :

தேவடோனடகன் லன்செல்வன்மறறடறன்மரும்
பாலையயேஙாற்றன ள்பாரினமற்றென்மரும்
இநதாமணி - கனகமாவல்யாரிலமபகம - ாஅ்ய்சு - கவி.

Some said, that king is a deity and no man; other said, a (meritorious) penance hath his wife performed in the world.

Here, எனமரும் stands for எனபாரும். So Pavan'anti, in his Nannùl, often has எனமருமுஊடோ, *there are some who say, &c.*

XXXIII. To the remarks on the indicative of the negative verb, contained in No. 14 of the other grammar, I have here to add:

First: That the third person neuter singular may reject து : as, கடவா, செயயா, ஆகா. By adding வன் to these, we have the plural: as, ஆகவன், கடவாவன், செயயாவன், திரியாவன்.

Secondly: In forming the negative, it is common to use the appellatives இல்லன், அல்லன், of which we have spoken in rule XIV. The compound, which is conjugated through all the persons, is obtained, by affixing those appellatives, either to the imperative of the positive, or to the participle preterite: as, நானேபேசல்லேல்லன : or more frequently with a single ல், பேசேலன; நீபேசலி; அவனபேசலன; அவனபேசல்ல்; அததேபேசல்து; காமபேசடேலம, or பேசலம்; சீர்பேசலிர்; அவர்பேசலர்; அலைபேசல், or அலைபேசலன : thus, உணடிடேலன, உணடிலி, உணடிலன, உணடிலன, &c.

———⊕———

SECTION THE SECOND.

OF THE IMPERATIVE.

XXXIV. In addition to my remarks on the imperative, called எவல், which are given in No. 68 of the other grammar, I shall here notice certain peculiarities of that mood in this dialect.

First: உ is scarcely ever affixed to the imperative, except it be joined to a rough letter: as, அடக்கு, வாங்கு, விடு, where the உ remains. Hence, while, in common Tamil, we write உணறு, இனறு, சொலது, &c. in this dialect, we use உண், இன், சொல், &c.

Secondly: By adding மோ to the above, we have another form for the second person singular: thus, உண் becomes உண்மோ; உவா, உவாமோ; கேள், கேன்மோ; சொல், சொன்மோ. In the two last instances, ள் and ல், being followed by ம, are changed to ன் and ன, respectively.

Thirdly: By adding இ to the same abbreviated imperative, we get a third form for the second person singular; and by adding தீர், one for the plural: thus, from அருள, அருளி; and from போ, போதி. However, I have never seen கேளி formed from கேள்; the word becoming கேட்டி, on account of the meeting of ள் and த: so, for the plural கேட்டீர், போதீர், &c. In the Ràmàyan'am of Camben, a devotee named Gaudamen, discovering that his wife Agaligei had yielded to the impure embraces of the god Dévéndren, curses her with this imprecation; *become stone.* The passage is,

மெல்லியலாளோநோக்கிவில்லிமகளவண்ணயீயுறை
கல்லியலாதியென்று   என
பாலகாண்டம - அகதிகைப்படலம - ன, கவி.

Looking on the slender formed (Agaligei) *he said, oh thou who art like to a mercenary strumpet, be thou transformed to a stone!* Where ஆதி is the imperative of the verb அதல *to become.* Observe, that we must not add the terminations இ and தீர் to வா and தா, but to வரு and தரு, which would be the regular imperative, according to the general rule.

The last mentioned form is also used for the second person singular of the preterite: thus, a certain poet has, விந்தியெறகெடுதி, *if you have dismissed* (him,) *you have ruined* (yourself.) Another author has, கோகனாறுபோனிஎ *thou wentest without seeing.* This must not be condemned, as being either obscure or absurd: in Latin, *veni* is both the second person singular of the imperative, and the first person singular of the preterite; *sequere* is the second person singular, both of the imperative, and of the present; and *amare* is, at the same time, the second person singular of the imperative passive, the second person singular of the present passive, and the infinitive active. Many other instances might be adduced. This double use of the same word is not productive of any ambiguity.

Fourthly: It is still more common to use the second persons singular and plural of the negative verb, for the second persons singular and plural of the imperative positive: as, கேளாய *hear thou*; கேளீா *hear ye*. It is of consequence to attend to this use of the word; for I can state from experience, that, until I became acquainted with it, it gave me no small trouble.

XXXV.. The second person plural, besides the forms already specified, as கேட்டீர், விற்றீர், சொல்லிர், வாரீர், கூறீர், &c. has the following:

First: The following terminations, மின், மினீர், மிறீஏ, correspond, in the plural, with the singular termination மோ: (see XXXIII.) thus, உண்மின, உண்மினீர், உண்மிஏ, கேளாமின, கேளாமினீர், கேளாமிஏ, விடுமின, விடும்வீர், விடும்ஏ, போமின, போமீனீர், போம்ஏ, செ ன்மின், சென்மினீர், சென்மிஏ.

Secondly: The same person may also be formed by affixing these terminations to the common imperative in உ: as, சொல்லுமின், செல்லு மின், வாழுமின். But from வா and தா are formed வம்மின், தம்மின. Thus much of the imperative positive.

XXXVI. The prohibitive of the common dialect, as செய்யாதே, மிறி யாதே, is rarely used; but this mood is formed:

First: By adding to the imperative positive, செய், மிறி, சொல், &c. the terminations அற்க for the singular, and அற்கிர் for the plural. Example:

வியவற்கவெளுஞான்றுநந்தனவிை
நயவற்கனதிடயவாவி   வை
திருவ-சமி, அதி-க, குற.

Think not highly of thyself at any time, neither delight thou in deeds which bring not forth good fruit.

Secondly: By adding to the same word the termination எல், for the

singular: as, செயடேல, (*) பிரிடேயல, சொல்லேல, (†) அடைடேயல.
Thus, in the poem entitled Bàradam, we have:

ஆதவடேனமுனிடேயடெல்லஹண்யாளுடையானவடேனமுனிடேயல்
எாதவடேனமுனிடேயிதயத்திகிருப்பவடேனமுனிடேயல்
மாதவடேனமுனிடேயல்மதவெங்கனலானவடேனமுனிடேயல்
நீதவடேனமுனிடேயல்முனிடேயடெலனதின்றுபணிந்தனடோ

இருட்டினன்றூதுசருககம் - டாருடசா -கவி.

O thou, who art the sun, be not angry! Thou, who hast me for thy servant, be not angry! Thou whose penance is rewarded, be not angry! Thou who dwellest in my heart, be not angry! O thou husband of Latchimi, be not angry! Thou fire of intense heat, be not angry! Thou righteous one, be not angry, be not angry! So saying, they stood and worshipped him.

Thirdly. By adding மின் to the negative in ஆ, for the plural: as, இராமின, செயயாமின.

Fourthly. It is also very common to form the plural of the prohibitive by affixing மின் to the verbal in ல; (see No. XXV.) this letter being changed to ன், on account of the ம which follows: thus, from பாடல் *to sing*, comes பாடன்மின்; from விடல *to leave*, விடனமின்; from கூறல *to say*, கூறனமின; from சொல்லல, சொல்லனமின. Hence, சொன்மின or சொலுமின, means *say ye*; while சொல்லன்மின means *say ye not*. Thus, from அகலல *to depart*, அகன்மின is formed from the imperative அகல், and has a positive sense, *depart ye*; but அகலன்மின is formed from the verbal அகலல், and has a prohibitive sense, *depart ye not*. Example:

தூதன்னவணச்சுனியன்மிடென ரு
வேதம்முதருதன்விலைககினரு ல்

இரா - அதிகாய - பட - சசு, கவி.

The first Lord of the Védàs checked them, saying, be not ye angry against him who is a messenger.

(*) பிரிதல to be separated.

(†) அடைதல் to obtain.

Here, from the verbal சினியல் *to be angry*, we have சினியன்மின *be ye not angry*.

Fifthly, and lastly. As இ is the termination of the singular positive; so மோ, added to the verbal in ல், as in the last rule, is the termination of the singular negative: thus, செய்யன்மோ, பாடன்மோ.

<hr/>

SECTION THE THIRD.
OF THE INFINITIVE.

XXXVII. Of the infinitive mood we have treated in No. 70 and 133 of the other grammar: I shall here add a few remarks.

First. In this dialect, the same verb has, in the infinitive, several terminations: as, நடக்க, நடப்ப; அடிக்க, அடிப்ப; துணிய, துணிச, துணிகுப; செய்ய, செய்க, செய்குப; காண, காங்க, காணிய; வாழு, வாழிய; போக, போவ, போகுப; ஆக்க, ஆக்குக; நோக்க, நோககுக.

When an infinitive, differing from the usual form, terminates in single க; as, துணிக, செய்க, ஆக்குக, it does not double a following rough letter, as it would in other cases. Example:

எண்ணித்துணிக்கருமநதுணிநதபி
னெனஎறுவெமெனபதிருக் கு

இருவ-சயிள-அதி, எ - குறஎ.

Consider before you resolve on a weighty action.
To resolve and say, we will consider hereafter, is an error.
Another poet has

ஆகுவதுனைதனிலறததையாக்கு க
போகுவதுனைதனிலெவகுளிபோகு க
நோகுவதுனைதனிலருானநோகு க
காகுவதுனைதனிலவிாதஙகாக்க வெ

If there be aught worthy to be done—do charity.
If there be aught that should be avoided—avoid anger.
If there be aught that should be regarded—regard virtue.
If there be aught that should be observed—observe rites.

Secondly. We stated, in the other grammar, that the infinitive may be used for the imperative, but that it expresses entreaty, rather than command. Pavan'anti in his Nannùl, after making the same remark, adds, that, in the higher dialect, when the infinitive is used in this way for any person, gender or number of the imperative, it denotes wish rather than command, being the form which we employ to express any desire of the mind. Hence, it answers to the present of the optative, a mood which does not exist in Tamil. Thus, பொறுகத்தையகான் *may I bear the evil!* சீபெறு க *mayest thou obtain!* நானவாழ்க *may I live!* நீவாழ்க *mayest thou live!* நீனறந்தைதவாழ்க *may thy father live!* அறக்கினைபுகழேழ *may thy praise be celebrated!* நாபெவிஅக *may we be manifest!* சீகொபொரிய *approach ye!* அவோதுணிக *may they be daring!* அதுவேவருக *may that come!* அவை பெயழுகக *may those things become customary!* Here, the infinitive has been used for every person number and gender of the imperative. Thus, also, நானவாழிய *may I live!* நீவாழிய *mayest thou live!* இறைவனவா ழிய *may the king live!* நமர்வாழிய *may our people live!*

To the infinitive, thus used, ர் is sometimes added, as, நானவாழியர், நீவாழியர்.

Thirdly. The infinitive is also used for the gerund, as shall be explained in the proper place.

XXXVIII. I shall here notice particularly the infinitive எனை, or என, from the verb எனல *to say;* the word being very frequently used in this dialect.

First. It is used for எனறு: as, வநதாயெனச்சொனனனை *he said that thou camest;* இவனுஒன்சொலவனெய *say thou who he is.* This use, as I shall hereafter explain, it has in common with other verbs.

Secondly. Affixed to certain words, which cannot be used alone, it gives them an adverbial signification: as, திகெனை-பொடடெனை-வெ யடதன *swiftly.*

Thirdly. It denotes comparison: as, செஞ்சுடொனவிளஙகினுனை *he shone so, that he might be called the red sun:* i. e. *he shone like the red sun.* Thus, மாடெனவளர்நதான *he grew like a tree.* In this sense, it may be joined to the gerund of the preterite: as, கொழிப்ழ்நதனை

ழ்ந்தாள் *she fell as a creeper falls* (unsupported) புகிபாயநெதனனச்சி னந்துவநதான *he came furious as a bounding tyger*. Thus, instead of (*) கடிததாற்போல, (†) நகைததாற்போல, we may say either கடிததெத ன், நகைததெதன், as above; or கடிததாடென், நகைததாடென்.

Fourthly. The word என, or also எனு, is used for the conjunction உம், *and:* thus, நீயெனவ்வெனன்: with a verb; as நீயெனவ்வெனனவந்தீர், நகெனெருத்தாவெனைபடோடாவாம்: thus, தம்மெனைச்சாத்தனெனையபொச ம்மனெனைழுவரும்வநதார். In this way we may also use எனது and எனறு, gerunds of the same verb: as, நீயெனது தம்மெனை நிருவரும்போயின், தம்மெனைறுடொயாமமனெனறுவகனறுர்.

Lastly. Observe, that the infinitive ஆக is frequently contracted by syncope to ஆ: thus, a certain author has, அருடேயுடெலாவெறடேனயுயிஞா க்டெகாணைடான, literally, *He took benevolence as a body, and virtue as the soul.*

SECTION THE FOURTH.

OF PARTICIPLES.

XXXIX. Concerning the participles, பெயடெச்சம, I have some rules to add to those which are given in No. 72 and 73 of the other grammar.

First. As there are three forms for the present tense of the verb, so are there three corresponding forms for the present participle: as, நடக்கிற, நடக்கினற, நடவாகினற.

Secondly. When the preterite of a verb terminates in இடென, the preterite participle generally ends in இய: as, (‡) அடக்கிய, (§) டேவண டிய.

Thirdly. The participle of the future is expressed, as was mentioned in the other grammar, by the third person neuter singular of the future

---

(*) கடிததல் to bite.
(†) நகைததல் to laugh.
(‡) அடக்கல் to restrain.
(§) டேவணடல் to intreat.

tense, which person always ends in உம்: thus, செய்யும், (*) நிமிரும், நடக்கும், வாழும். In the superior dialect, when this word is used as the participle, it may always drop the ம்: as, செய்யு, நிமிரு. In this case, if the following word begins by a vowel, உ also is cut off: as, எதிர்பரப்பிரவி *the beam-spreading sun*, for எதிர்பரப்புயிரவி, unless the participle consist of two short syllables, like (†) வரு, (‡) தரு, (§) பொரு, from வரும், தரும், பொரும்.

The உ may also be dropped though the following word do not begin by a vowel, provided the consonant to which it is joined, be among the finals: thus, நிமிர்கொமபு, வாழ்குடி. This syncope cannot, however take place, if the உ be preceded by one syllable only, short by nature, and not containing a double consonant: thus, for வரும we may use வரு, but not வர், although ர் is a final; but for வாரும, from the verbal வார்த்தல் *to pour*, we may use வார், since the உ is preceded by a long syllable. Accordingly, we constantly find the word ஆர் used, not for the pronoun *who*, but for the participle ஆரும், from the verb ஆர்தல் *to be filled*, whence it is aptly rendered by the adjective *full*.

But if the consonant to which உ is joined, be a final, and be doubled, the உ is dropped, together with its consonant, although it be preceded by one syllable only, and that short by nature: thus, from (‖) வெல்லும, வெல்; from (¶) உண்ணும, உண்; from செய்யும, செய்; from (**) துள ரும, துள; from (††) தும்மும, தும்.

Finally. If the consonant joined with உ be ய, preceded by more than one syllable, it may be dropped, together with the உ, even though it be not doubled: thus, from அணியுங்கலன - அணிகலன; from புரியுந்தலைய - புரிதலைய; from அறியுமபொருள - அறிபொருள. But (‡‡) சாயும and (§§) காயும from சாய், and காய cannot drop the ய also, and become சா, கா; because,

---

(*) நிமிர்தல் to stand erect or straight.

(†) வருதல் to come.

(‡) தருதல் to give.

(§) பொருதல் to fight.

(‖) வெல்லல் to conquer.

(¶) உண்ணல் to eat.

(**) துளளல் to leap.

(††) தும்மல் to sneeze.

(‡‡) சாய்தல் to decline.

(§§) காயதல் to become dry.

although the preceding syllable be long, there is one only. **Observe, that** அனி and காய், with similar words, are also nouns; and that, when prefixed adjectively to other nouns, they double a following rough letter; which is not the case when they are used as participles: thus, அணிக்கலன means *a beautiful necklace,* அணிகலன *a necklace which adorns:* காய்க்கொம்பு is, *a bough having fruit;* காய்கொம்பு *a withering bough.*

Fourthly. The participle of the negative verb terminates in அ or த, as stated in the other grammar: thus, செயயா or செயயாத.

XL. It was stated, in the other grammar, that the participle future is used likewise for the participle present. I have here to add, that it may also be put for the participle preterite. Thus, in Nannûl (Part II. Chap. 3, Rule 13) the author remarks, that பொருங்களம for instance, may, according to the context, signify, either பொருகினறகளம *the plain where they fight;* பொருதகளம *the plain where they fought;* or பொ ருங்களம *the plain where they will fight.* In that stanza of Chintâman'i, which was so fully explained in No. XXIII, we met with உளடு, used for உளடும, and contracted by syncope in உளடடாகது, on account of the following vowel. This word is the participle future; but as it was followed in the sentence by உணட, a participle preterite, it, likewise, had the force of a participle preterite; being put for உளடடிஎ.

XLI. From any participle we may form verbals in து, as was stated in the other grammar, No. 107. I have here to add:

First. That these verbals terminate, in the plural, in வை (*) or எ: thus, செயகினறவை, or செயகினறஎ; செயதவை, or செயதஎ; செயவ வை, or செயவஎ. So also the negatives, செயயாதவை, or செயயாதஎ; as also செயயாரவஎ. They may also terminate in simple அ, as was stated in No. XIII. of this grammar: செயகினற, செயத, செயவ.

Secondly. That the future verbal, in particular, is much used, in conjunction with the verb ஆதல், *to become,* in forming compound verbs. Such are நவிலவதாஞஎ *he said,* for நவினறுஎ, செயவதாஏஎ for செய தஎ *I did,* செயவதவாஎ for செயவாஎ *he will do.*

_____

(*) The termination is not வை, but ஐ; the வ being inserted by the rules of ortho= graphy: thus செயகினற - ஐ, செயகினறவை.

SECTION THE FIFTH.

OF GERUNDS.

XLII. Of gerunds, (விணெயெச்சம,) we have treated in the grammar of the common Tamil, No. 71. There are several remarks to be added, which relate to this dialect.

The விணெயெச்சம is not exclusively a gerund, being applied to any part of the verb which is not conjugated by persons, except the participles; and although I have thought fit to include all these words under the term gerund, yet, as they are of every tense, they cannot all be rendered by the gerunds of the Latins. Concerning gerunds, the author of Nannùl says; (Rule 24, on the verb.)

செய்துசெயபுசெயயாசசெயயூசசெயெதனச
செயசசெயின்செயயியசெயயியர்வான்பான்
பாகருவிணெயெச்சமபிறவைநதொானறு
முககாலமுமுமுறைதரும

(Of the following) *gerunds* (the first) *five* (the following) *one* (and the remaining) *six belong to the three tenses in the order of succession :* that is, according to the order in Tamil grammars, the first five செய்து- செயபு-செயயா-செயயூ-செயெதன் appertain to the past; the sixth செய to the present; and the remainder செயின செயயிய-செயயியர்-வான-பான- பாகரு- to the future.

The following remarks will explain this rule :

XLIII. First. Of the twelve words here enumerated, the first five are gerunds of the preterite.

1st, செய்து. This is the form used in common Tamil: thus, செய்து, படித்து, அடக்கி; எணணி.

2d, செயபு. This is obtained by adding பு to the common form of the imperative: thus, from (*) இறு is formed இறுபு; from உண், உண்பு; from (†) வாழ்த்தது, வாழ்த்ததுபு ; from அடக்கு, அடக்குபு; which words have

_____

(*) இறல to be severed as a chain, rope, &c. (†) வாழ்த்ததல to praise.

the same force as செய்து, இறறு உண்டு, &c. The verbs வருதல், தருதல், however, do not form this gerund from their imperatives வா, தா, but from வரு and தரு, which would regularly be their imperatives according to the general rule: thus, வருபு, தருபு, for வந்து, தந்து.

3d, செயயா. This is the negative, (see No. XXX.) and is used for the positive gerund, in the same way as we stated எறு to be used for எனறு: thus, (*) எழா for எழுந்து; உன்ணு for உண்டு; கூறு for கூறி. Example:

என்டுறவிடை நல்கயிடைஎருஇயெழா
வன்றுள்வயிரசிஹ்கைகக்கொடுஉான்
பொன்ஞுழ்கஉசமபடுதாழுகிகி
னின்றுஞிமையெயார்கஉணளிநதனால்
இரா - அதிகா - வதைபயட - மஉ,கவி.

Permission being thus given to him, he made obeisance; and arising, he grasped his well-strung adamantine bow, and clothing himself in his coat of golden mail, stood in semblance as a (threatening) *cloud.—The never-slumbering* (gods) *trembled.*

The poet is relating, that Adicàyen, having obtained permission from Ràvan'en, his father, rises up, seizes his arms, and prepares for battle. In this passage, எழா is used for எழுநது, and புகுதா (†) for புகுந்து. புகா &c. may be used in the same sense.

4th, செயயு. This is used for செயது: thus, எழு, உன்ணு, &c. but this is inelegant.

5th, செய்தென். This is obtained by affixing the word என to the common form of the preterite gerund; as, உகதென், படிததென்; which have the same force as வநது, படிதது. We stated in No. XXXIII. that the word என is used to denote comparison: hence, the foregoing examples may also be rendered by வந்ததுபோல, படித்ததுபோல.

The verbal in ல், with the addition of உம், is not unfrequently used for the preterite gerund: thus, for கேட்டு, கேட்டலும்; for சொலலி, சொல்லலும்; for செயது, செயயலும்; for படிதது, படிததலும்; &c.

Respecting the use of the preterite gerund, I have to remark: first,

_____

(*) எழுதல் to arise.　　　(†) புகுதல் to enter.

that, when it ends in உ, as செயது, செயபு, வநது, வருபு it is usual to affix the words உள் or உழ், which signify *place*: thus, செயதுள், செயதுழ், செயபுள், வநதுள், &c. These compounds have the same force as the expressions used in common Tamil, செயதபோது, வநதபோது, &c. which, referring to time, are rendered *when I did, thou didst, he did*; and, referring to cause, *whereas I did*, &c. Secondly, that the particle அறது, which is the same as போல, is frequently added to this gerund: thus, ஆடியறது, வநதற்று, for ஆடினதுபோனறது, வந்ததுபோனறது. Example:

தீயவைசெயதார்கெடுதனிழறன்வீன
யாநதடியுறஙதற் று.

திருவ - உச, அதி - அ, குற.

Here, உறஙதற்று is used for உறஙததுபோல.

The meaning is: *Destruction follows evil doers even as the shadow unceasing presses on the steps of it's* (substance.)

Finally. Besides the forms used in common Tamil, such as செய்யாது, செய்யாமல்; in this dialect, we may also employ, for the negative gerund, words similar to செய்யாமை; which I stated in the other grammar, No. 177, to be properly a kind of negative verbal, and to be used as a noun. Thus, a poet, describing the streets of a certain city, says: நூலெனவுழானைகடேயாடி *running, as a string, without curve.*

XLIV. Secondly. The gerund of the present has only one form, செய், written also செய்ய, which is the infinitive already treated of. It is aptly rendered by the ablative absolute of the Latins, as I observed in No. 120 of the other grammar: thus, நானகெட்கச்சொனனைன *me audiente dixit, -he said it in my hearing*; நீகாணைசெய்தான *te vidente fecit, he did it in thy sight.* Thus Tiruvaḷuven, speaking of hospitality, says:

மோப்பக்குழையுமனிச்சழுகந்திரிந்து
நோக்கக்குழையும்விருங் து.

திருவ - கூ, அதி - ய, குற.

அனிச்சம் is the name of a flower remarkable for it's delicacy; on which account, the poet says:

The Anicham flower languishes when it's fragrance is inhaled, the feast languishes when the countenance (of the host) is averted.

In this passage, the words செய்ப்பு, and நோக்க, are used as gerunds of the present.

Further, we learn from Nannùl, that this infinitive may also be used for the future gerund; it then answers to the future participle in *rus*, of the Latins, as was explained in the other grammar, No. 123: thus, பின்பிதைக்காணவப்பின் *venite postea hoc visuri,--come ye after, to see this.*

XLV. Thirdly. Besides the infinitive, which, as I have just said, may serve for the future gerund, the author of Nannùl assigns to this gerund six other forms:

1st. செயின், that is, the several forms of the conditional; as, எனறுல், எனனில், ஏனில், என்ன, செய்தால், செய்யில, செயின்; respecting the formation of which mood, see No. 115 of the other grammar. In this dialect, the forms in இல் or இன், as செயயில, செயயின, are those most in use. There is another form of the conditional, which is obtained by adding ஆல் or எல் to any person of any tense of the verb, or to verbals in து: thus, செய்கின்றேறுல், or செய்கின்றற்னெல, செயதஹணேயல், செயகுவனேல், செயகுவமெல, செயதின்னோல, &c. Thus, likewise, செயகின்றறுதெல், செயதுதெல், செயவுதெல். We may also, drop the து, and write செய்கினறவால், செயதவால், செயவவால்; or செயகிறறைனவால செயதனவால செயவனவால், &c. The conditional is termed a future gerund, because, from the nature of a condition, it imports an action which has not taken place, nor is actually in progress, and which, consequently, is hereafter to happen: as, *If I shall salt it, it will be purified.* Thus a certain poet has, தாம்வெண்ணடினல்குளர்காதலர் *the benevolent will give, if necessary, even their own selves.*

2d. செயயிய. This is formed by affixing the termination இய to the imperative: thus, from கண், காணிய; from செய், செயயிய; (*) from செல, செலகிய; &c. This also answers to the participle in *rus*, of the

(*) The ய being doubled, according to the rules of orthography.

Latins: இப்புதுமைகாணியவம்மின, *venite visuri, hoc portentum,--come to behold this wonder*, &c.

3d. செயயியர். This form is obtained by affixing the consonant ர் to the second form just mentioned: thus, காணியர், வாழியர், செயயியர், &c. and the force of both is the same. These two varieties of the future gerund do not, however, suit all verbs, as practice will more clearly evince.

4th வானே.
5th பானே. } The forms represented by the two foregoing terminations, are the same as the third person masculine singular of the future, செயயவானே, அணிவானே, நடபபானே, படிபபானே. But when they serve as future gerunds, they are used in every person, number, and gender; and, like the other forms, may be rendered by the Latin participle in *rus*: thus, உனைபபானே, வந்தேன, வந்தாய், வந்தான, வந்தாள், &c. thus, இதைசசெய வானுனைவிளிதேன *I called thee to do this*. This form is not unusual in this dialect, and is common to all verbs.

6th. பாகு. This termination, added to the imperative, gives the last form of the future gerund: as உண்பாகு, காண்பாகு, தருபாகு: thus, செல்வந்தருபாகுச்சென்றனை *venit daturus felicitatem,--he came to bestow happiness.* I have very rarely, however, met with this form.

SECTION THE SIXTH.

APPENDIX.

XLVI. The preceding part of this work is a brief selection from the precepts which, in the copious treatise of Pavananti, occupy no less than 456 rules. This will, I trust, suffice to pave the way for the Student, to enable him to comprehend the greater part of what he will read, and to facilitate his further enquiries.

The remarks on syntax, contained in the other grammar, are equally applicable here. The chief peculiarities of the superior dialect, in this respect, were noticed, in treating of the noun and the verb.

The nature of மரபு, that is, *propriety and beauty of style*, is thus defined by Pavananti :

எபபொருடெசடெசகிடெனவவாறுயிர்கடொர்
செயவினாப்படிடெசபபுதனமா   இப.

நன - டெசால் - பொறு - நஎ, ரூ.

To speak of similar matter, with like expression, and in the same style, as sages have spoken, this is propriety of speech.

It will, therefore, be worth while for those who study this dialect, to attend diligently to the practice of ancient authors. I propose, in this appendix, to specify some instances in which these writers vary from the rules laid down in this grammar.

First. The த்து is sometimes struck out, by syncope, from the dative case of a noun ending in ம் ; so that for கிலத்துகு we find கிலகு : thus, in Chintàmani, I have seen, கயகு put for கயத்துகு. The passage is :

தண்கயகுறறமுபொதுநதாழகிவஷையிநதவியும
வன்டெகாடிடெகாயததூவு   ம.

பதுமையாரிலமடகம - எசு, கவி.

Flowers brought from the cool tanks, flowers gathered from the pendant branches, and flowers plucked from the graceful creepers.

Secondly. Besides the regular forms, already noticed, the word அறம் sometimes has for it's appellative அறடெவார், and for it's adjective அற விய, (*) In Chintàmani we have, அறவியமனததராகி, &c.

Thirdly. Instead of the usual termination of the future, டெகன் is sometimes used : thus, டெசயடெகன for டெசயடெவன, அடைகடெகன for அடைபடெபன : so in Chintàmani எனனுனைகடெகடெகு, எனடெசயடெகடெகு, *what shall I say, what shall I do!* Another poet has : இடிகடடைடெபரி டெதனடெகடெகுடெவனறுயிர்டெபரிடெதனடெகடெகு *shall I say that the roaring sea, or my grief is the greater.*

Fourthly. We have stated, that the infinitive, which always terminates in அ, serves for every person of either number of the imperative. Some-

_____

(*) விசயமாடெதவியார்துறவு - உசுச - கவி.

times, however, the infinitive, thus used, is made to terminate in உ, instead of அ: thus, in Chintàmani, we find, எந்தையார்க்கெழுகென்றான he said to his parents, arise! Here, எழுகு is put for எழுக, which is used in the same sense as எழுமின.

Fifthly. We have stated that செய்யின், கிளக்கின், &c. may be used for செய்தல், கிளத்தல், &c.; and செய்யினும், கிளக்கினும் &c. for செய்தாலும், கிளத்தாலும், &c. In ancient writers, we find செய்யின, கிளப்பின, which are formed from the future, used in the same sense: thus, in Chintàmani, we have, கிளப்பினுமடங்கித்தழுவமம.

Sixthly. In ancient writers, I have frequently seen the verbal in ல், with the addition of ஆ, used for the negative gerund, or participle: thus, the author of Silappadicàram, writes யாவதுங்கிளையலா, for கிளையாது, which means *without considering;* thus, Tiruvalluver, (௩, அதி - ௬ குற.) செயற்கரியசெய்கலாதார், where செய்கலாதார், is used for செய்யாதார். In Chintàmani, (*) we even find கவிறருதார், for கவில்லதார், from the verb கவில், *to say*.

Seventhly. Instead of ஆன், the termination of the third person, masculine singular, you will sometimes meet with ஆன: thus, Camben, in his Ràmàyanam, in the chapter intitled அதிகாயன்வதை, has:

கண்டானனவிராமனெனுங்களி மா
வுண்டாடியவெங்களனூடுருவ ப்
புண்டானுறுநெஞ்சுபுழுக்கமுற த்
திண்டாடினன்வந்தசினத்திறலோன

உயிர, கவி.

The furious hero (Adicáyen) *advancing, viewed the battle-field where Ramen, like a raging elephant, had sported in destruction—and with aching heart, began the fight, to be yet more oppressed.*

In the same work, a few stanzas further on:

என்றனவிராவணனுக்கிளைய யா
னன்றுகவிதென்றுருநாயகனும

Thus spoke the younger brother of Ràvanen. It is well, replied the chief.

(*) கேமசரியாரிலம்பகம் - ௫௬, கவி.

In these passages, we must read *candána* (*) *enrána*, for *candán enrán*. There are many instances like these, which, as they are merely anomalies, I thought it better to advert to here, than to specify them under the heads to which they severally belong.

XLVII. In this dialect, there are a variety of particles, or interjections.

First. Of these particles, some have a meaning, and will be found in their proper places in the dictionary. One of them, ந *na*, I shall here notice. This particle is explained, in Nannùl, (†) to signify some good quality. It is prefixed to substantives only. If the following letter be a consonant, it is doubled, of what class soever it may be; and if it be a vowel, double வ must be interposed: thus, நக்குடம் - நப்பொருள் - நல் வகை - நவ்வழி - நவ்வமிர்தம்.

Secondly. Others have no meaning, and are termed, on this account, அசைசொல், or உரையசை; under which head, they will be found in the dictionary. For instance, ஆல், which we have stated, in No. XLV. to be used for ஆகுல், is sometimes a mere expletive: as, அவகுடுஎ்கடெவனில், வருமாடொவொடெவனில்; as also கேட்டியால; which are put for அவடிருடெவ னில், வருடுமாடெவனில், கேட்டி, or கேசன். In like manner, the word ஒரும் is without meaning, and is used only to complete the verse. Example;

அருசுவடெதாருமறடெனடெயாருவஷி
யஞ்சிப்படெதாரும   வச

திருவ-உமஎ,அதி-சு,குற.

The fear of deceitful lusts is virtue.

In this passage, ஒரும் occurs twice, and in both cases is a mere expletive. In the same way, the following words are added, to complete the harmony of the verse, occasionally in the middle, but more frequently at the end, of a line: எ, அடொரா, அமம, அமமா, அனடெகு, அனடெற, மாடெதா, மனடெகூ; all which are without meaning. In the verse வெண்பா, however, these are introduced only in the middle of a line, and never at the end.

(*) It accords better with the genius of the language, to suppose கஎரடானஎ to be the verb in its usual form, and the following word to be அவிராமன, compounded of the proper name இராமன், and the demonstrative pronoun அவ்; the வ், which, according to the usual orthography, should be doubled, being written single, according to a rule contained in No. V of this grammar.

(†) இடைசொல்லியல - உ, சூத்திரம்.

PART THE SECOND.

OF TAMIL POETRY.

XLVIII. A religious recluse, named Amirtasàcaren, as I observed in the introduction, wrote a work called Càricei (காசிகை) which, without treating of the art of poetry, merely contains the rules of Tamil versification. The word காசிகை has three significations; *a woman, embellishment,* and *a kind of verse,* commonly called கலித்துறை. The work is dedicated to a woman, to whom all his precepts are addressed; it treats of verse, which may be termed the embellishment of language; and is composed throughout in the-metre called கலித்துறை. On this threefold account, the author gave to his book the title abovementioned. In his introduction, he divides his subject into eight parts: viz. எழுத்தசை சீர் பந்தமடி தொடை பாவினம். First, எழுத்து, *letters.* Second, அசை, *syllables, considered with reference to feet.* Third, சீர், *feet.* Fourth, பந்தம், termed also தளை, *the connecting of feet with each other.* Fifth, அடி, *lines, of which a stanza is composed.* Sixth, தொடை, *the consonance of the lines in a stanza.* Seventh, பா, *the different kinds of stanza.* Eighth, இனம், *the subdivision of each kind.*

Of letters, enough has already been said: my first chapter, therefore, shall relate to feet, and the other requisites of verse; the second, to the different kinds of stanza; and the third, to the subdivisions of each kind. I shall add a fourth chapter, which shall contain a few remarks concerning the art of Tamil poetry.

CHAP. I.

SECTION THE FIRST.

அசை.

XLIX. The word அசை has various meanings; but is here used to signify syllables, considered with reference to metrical feet. Of அசை there are two kinds, நேரசை, and நிரையசை. நேர், among other significations, means *that which is single;* நிரை, *several things disposed in order.*

Hence, a *Gநரஞ* is one syllable only; and this must either be long by nature, or position; or, if short, must be the only syllable remaining, after the other *அஞ*, contained in the word to which it belongs, have been scanned. For example, in the word *கன்றுழ்*, *கன்* is a *Gநரஞ*; because, although the syllable *க* is short by nature, yet, it is followed by two consonants: *று* is a *Gநரஞ*, because it is long by nature; and *ழ்*, which is both short by nature, and without following consonants, is nevertheless considered as a *Gநரஞ*, because it is the only remaining syllable.

A *நிஞரயஞ*, always consists of two syllables, of which the first must be short, both by nature and by prosody, and the second may be either short or long. For instance, the word *வழி* is a *நிஞரயஞ*, of two short syllables; *மனம்* is a *நிஞரயஞ*, of which the first syllable is short, and the second is long by prosody; and *விழா* is a *நிஞரயஞ*, having the first syllable short, and the second by nature long. In this kind of *அஞ*, then, the first syllable only is considered. If that be short, and be followed by another syllable, in the same word, the two unite, to form a *நிஞரயஞ*: thus, in the word *விஞங்கி*, *விஞங்* is a *நிஞரயஞ*, and *இ*, which is a single and detached syllable, is a *Gநரஞ*. But in the word *விஞங்கிஞை*, since *இ* is not now a detached syllable, but is followed by another, in the same word, *இஞை* is a *நிஞரயஞ*, although it's last syllable is long. These observations respecting *அஞ*, since they differ from our ideas, and are essential to a knowledge of the Tamil prosody, demand particular attention.

SECTION THE SECOND.

சீர்.

L. Metrical feet are termed *சீர்.* The Tamils do not, like us, give to each kind of foot an arbitrary appellation; but, in order to have, in one word, both the designation and the example, they apply to each kind of foot the name of some tree, in which its quantity is exhibited. For instance, a foot consisting of two *Gநரஞ* is termed *Gதமா*, which is the name of a tree, and consists itself of two *Gநரஞ*: and so of the rest, as will hereafter appear.

There are thirty kinds of feet, which are divided into five classes. (*)

The first class contains those feet which consist of a single அசை, and which are, therefore, termed ஏரசைச்சீர. These are distinguished into நேரசை, which are called நாள், and நிளையசை, which are called மலர்.

We can seldom make use of this class, except at the close of the stanza called வெண்பா. To these feet we may add abbreviated உ, (குற்றியலுகரம்) and they are then termed, respectively, காசு and பிறப்பு. Sometimes, though rarely, உ without abbreviation (முற்றுகரம்) is added; but this can take place only when உ follows a soft or mediate letter, and not when it is joined to a rough one: as in the following குறள்வெண்பா:

எவ்வ - துறைவ - துலக - முலகெதெஜோ
டவ்வ - துறைவ - தறி   வு
இருவ - சாஉ, அஇ - சூ, குற.

It is wise to live in the world as the world lives.

The word அறிவு at the close of the stanza, consists of அறி, which is a நிளையசை, and of வு, in which the முற்றுகரம் is joined to the mediate letter வ.

LI. The second class contains those feet which consist of two அசை, and which are comprised under the term இயற்சீர். They are of four kinds. First, தேமா, composed of two நேர். Second, புளிமா, composed of one நிளை and one நேர். Third, கருவிளம், composed of two நிளை. Fourth, கூவிளம், composed of one நேர் and one நிளை.

LII. The third class contains those feet which consist of three அசை, of which the last is a நேரசை. They are included under the general appellation வெண்சீர். These also are of four kinds, which are formed by adding, to the several feet of the second class, a நேரசை expressed by the word காய்: First, தேமாவுகாய, composed of three நேர். Second, புளிமாவுகாய,

---

(*) In the native grammars, there are only four grand divisions, depending on the number of அசை; viz. அசைச்சீர், feet of one அசை; இயற்சீர், feet of two அசை; உரிசீர், feet of three அசை; பொாதச்சீர், feet of four அசை; so that வெண்சீர் and வருசச்சீர் are comprehended in the class உரிசீர்.

composed of one கிளை and two சேர். Third, கருவிளைகாய், composed of two கிளை and one சேர். Fourth, கூவிளைகாய், composed of a சேர், a கிளை, and a சேர்.

LIII. The fourth class contains those feet which consist of three அசை, of which the last is a நிரையசை, and these are comprised under the general term வஞ்சிச்சீர். They, likewise, are of four kinds, which are formed by adding to the several feet of the second class, a நிரையசை, expressed by the word கனி: First, தேமாங்கனி, composed of two சேர் and a கிளை. Second, புளிமாங்கனி, composed of a கிளை, a சேர், and a கிளை. Third, கருவிளைங்கனி, composed of three கிளை. Fourth, கூவிளைங்கனி, composed of one சேர் and two கிளை.

LIV. The fifth class contains those feet which consist of four அசை, and which are comprised under the general term போதுச்சீர். These are of sixteen kinds, which are formed: First, by adding to the several feet of the second class, two நேரசை, expressed by the word தண்பு: as, தேமாநதண்பு, புளிமாநதண்பு. Secondly, by adding a கிளா and a சேர், termed நறுமபு: as, தேமாநறுமபு. Thirdly, by adding a சேர் and a கிளா, termed தணணிழல் : as, தேமாநதணணிழல், Fourthly, by adding two கிளா, termed நறுகிழல்: as தேமாநறுகிழல்.

These sixteen kinds of feet are but little used.

LV. In the use of the Tamil feet, there is a peculiarity which I think it proper to notice. In Latin, a verse would be considered loose, and devoid of harmony, if each word in it were a distinct foot: the feet of a verse, therefore, are so disposed, that, in scanning, the words are run into each other, and concatenated like the links of a chain. The cadence of the Tamil verse, on the contrary, requires, that, not only in singing, but even in reading, the close of each foot should be marked by a slight pause : so that, to read a verse, and *to scan,* (அல்கிடை)are one and the same thing. Hence, although a Tamil foot may consist of several whole words, yet no word can be divided, as among the Latins, so as to belong, partly to one foot, and partly to another. This is the reason, why a short syllable, which remains alone at the end of a word, after scanning the அசை which precede it, cannot be joined with one of the syllables of the next word, and form a கிளையசை; but, from it's being a detached syllable, must, as already stated, be considered a நேரசை. However, the remaining syllable of one word may be united with the following word, provided that this be preserved entire, and, in conjunction with the first, constitute exactly one foot. For example, in the word தந்தபொருள், தந் is a நேரசை; த, which being a final syllable, might be reckoned alone as a நேரசை, may here be joined with பொ, and form a கிளையசை; and ருள் is a நேரசை: the two words, therefore, constitute one foot, of the kind termed கூவிள வகாய். In the verse வெண்பா, this deviation from the general rule rarely takes place. If the example had been தந்தபொருபுபன, we could not then have divided the word பொருபுபன, taking தந்தபொ ா ருப் for a கூவி ளகாய், and reserving பன to form part of another foot; but தந்த must have been considered a தேமா, and பொருபுபன a புளிமா.

There is, however, one species of verse, very rarely used, in which, as I shall hereafter explain, the words may be divided.

The terminations of cases, persons, and appellatives, are considered as distinct from the radical word, and may therefore, form part of a following foot: for instance, ஐ may be detached from மகன்னை, என from தந தேன, and ஆன from மகியான.

SECTION THE THIRD.

தளை

LVI. தளை or பாகதம், is the term used to express the manner in which feet are connected to form a line. பாகதம், among other significations, means *affinity;* and தளை means *fetters.* This *connexion* affects only the last அசை of one foot, and the first of that which immediately follows.

The first mode of connexion is அகியதத்தளை; so termed, because, as we shall presently perceive, it is peculiar to the verse called அகிசியபபா. It is used with the feet of the second class, இயற்சீர்; which must be so united, that a foot ending in a நேரசை, shall be followed by one beginning with a நேரசை; or, that a foot ending in a கிளையசை, shall be followed by one beginning with a நிரையசை. Thus, a தேமா, or a புளிமா, must be followed by a தேமா, or a கூவிளம் ; and a கருவிளம், or a கூவிளம், by a புளிமா, or a கருவிளம்.

LVII. The second mode of connexion is termed வெண்டளை, from it's being proper to the verse வெண்பா. It applies to the feet of the second and third classes, இயற்சீர், and வெண்சீர்; which are united according to the following rule. மாமுன்னிரையுமவிளைமுன்னேனருகுகாயமுன்னேனரும்.

The word முன் means *before*, but, according to our ideas of the position of words, it must be here translated *after*. The Tamils assert that, as the verse flows on, the reader leaves behind him the portion which he has read, and has before him the portion which remains: consequently, any word or foot is said to be *before* (முன்) any other which is not so far on in the line; and vice versâ. Thus, of the two words அயயாவருதி, அயயா is said to be behind, and அருதி to be before. I now proceed to explain the rule above quoted which must be understood in reference to the foregoing remark. First, மாமுன்னிரையும், that is, a foot ending in மா, of which there are two kinds, தேமா, and புளிமா, must be followed by one beginning with a நிரை; that is, by one of these four feet, புளிமா, புளிமாங்காய், கருவிளம், கருவிளங்காய். Secondly, விளைமுன்னேனரும், that is, a foot ending with a விளம், of which there are two kinds, கருவிளம், and கூவிளம், must be followed by one beginning with a தேர், that is, by one of these four feet; தேமா, தேமரகாய், கூவிளம், கூவிளங்காய். Thirdly, and lastly, காயமுன்னேனரும், that is, any of the four feet ending in காய், must be followed by one of these beginning with a தேர், which have just been mentioned.

LVIII. The third mode of connexion, கலித்தளை, is proper to the verse termed கலிப்பா; and is exactly the converse of that last mentioned: so that, where a நிரை follows in வெண்டளை, a தேர் follows here ; and where a தேர் follows in that, we shall have a நிரை in this.

LIX. The fourth mode of connexion, வஞ்சித்தளை, belongs to the verse called வஞ்சிப்பா. Besides the feet peculiar to it, which are those termed வஞ்சிச்சீர், it admits also those eight which belong to the second and third classes. This connexion requires, that all these feet should be united as in அஇரியதததன்; that is, that a சேர் should follow a சேர், and a கிணை a கிணை.

I shall here remark, what I shall have occasion to repeat, that the rules for connexion are strictly adhered to in the மெய்ப்பா alone, which must be composed in exact conformity to the rule of connexion வெண்டளை. The remaining modes of connexion, which occur in other kinds of verse, are by no means rigidly observed.

SECTION THE FOURTH.

அடி

LX. The word அடி expresses the individual lines which compose a stanza. The term பா, or பாட்டு, is not properly applied to a single verse, but signifies a stánza or a distich; since it always consists of more than one line, generally of four, but sometimes of two or three; as will hereafter appear.

There are five kinds of அடி, distinguished by the number of feet which they contain. 1st. A line consisting of two feet, called குறளடி. 2d. Of three, சிந்தடி. 3d. Of four, அளவடி. 4th. Of five, நெடிலடி. 5th. One containing more than five feet, whether six, seven, or more, is termed கழி நெடில் அடி.

LXI. In treating of the அடி, it is usual to consider it individually, and without reference to the stanza. The letter which begins a line, must begin one at least of the succeeding feet. Hence, this species of consonance is termed மோனை; that is, *commencement.* This is distinguished into several kinds, each of which has it's appropriate name. Thus, in the verse அளவடி, consisting of four feet, which is in frequent use and much esteemed, if this consonance fall on the second foot only, it is termed இணைமோனை; if on the third only, பொழிப்புமோனை; if on the fourth only, ஒருஉமோனை; if on the third and fourth, இடைந்தது வாய்மோனை; if on the second and fourth, இடைக்கதுவாய்மோனை; if on the second and third, கூழைமோனை: if on all the four feet, முற்றுமோ

ன. These distinctions are of little importance; but it is necessary to bear in mind, that the consonance must occur once at least in every அடி. If it comes in the middle of the line, or where there would naturally be a pause in reading, a better effect will be produced than if it falls elsewhere.

We stated, that the மோனை is the repetition of some letter. It is not, however, necessary, that the letters should be absolutely the same; it is sufficient if they be such as are considered to be consonous. The vowels which correspond in this respect, are அ, ஆ, ஒ, ஓள — இ, ஈ, எ, ஏ, and உ, ஊள, ஒ, ஓ. This property in the foregoing vowels is not affected by their junction with consonants; so that, க corresponds to கா, ஸெக, and கேள; கி, to கீ, கெ, and கே, &c. Of the consonants, த corresponds to ச, ஞ to ந, and ம to வ. Thus, in an அடி beginning with த, the consonance will be just, if, in the course of it, there occur a foot beginning with த, தா, ஸெத, or தேள; or even with ச, சா, ஸெச, or சேள: and conversely, in an அடி beginning with ச, &c. It was stated, (in No. II. fourth) that to words beginning with வ, இ may be prefixed; and therefore, although இ be not prefixed, the initial வ is still considered to be consonous with any of the following letters; வ, இ, ஈ, எ, ஏ.

———•⊙◉⊛◉⊙•———

SECTION THE FIFTH.

தொடை

LXII. தொடை is a word used to express things which are in any way connected regularly together; so that, *a chain,* which consists of united links; *a garland,* which is wreathed with flowers; *a necklace,* which is strung with pearls, may all be designated by the term தொடை. Hence, the word is also applied to that connexion, or consonance, which one அடி has with another in the same stanza. This is of various kinds; but that which is most in use, and which, indeed, can never be dispensed with, is named எதுகை. It requires, that the first foot of every line throughout a stanza should be consonous; and this consonance is considered to take place if, preserving uniformity in the quantity only of the

first syllable throughout the stanza, the second letter of each line be' of
the same class of letters and of the same quantity : (for the repetition of
the first letter is considered inelegant) but if the second letter, instead of
being merely of the same class, be identically the same, in each line, it is
esteemed a beauty.   Thus, if the first line begin with the word கருவி, I
must not commence another line in the same stanza with க; but, since க is
a short syllable, the other lines also must begin with a short syllable.
Again, since the second syllable is ரு, it will be a beauty if ரு begin the
second syllable in the other lines. This, however, is not absolutely necessary; it is enough if the second syllable be short, and begin with ர; so
that, the words இரவு, இரிபு, &c. contain an எதுகை to the word கருவி.

If, not only the second syllable of each line in the stanza, but the whole
of the first foot, with the exception of the first letter, be the same, the
verse is esteemed, in proportion to the difficulty of the performance.
Thus, if, where கருவி occurs in the first line, குருவி, அருவி, உருவி, &c.
come in the other lines, the verse will be particularly admired.

Example of a stanza beginning with a short syllable :

மணிபுகையரும்பியவான்மீன்வடிவொடுமலர்ந்து வென்முத்
தணிபுகைமணஸ்தொடென்பெய்யழகலான்றுவாடி-   த்
துணிபுனாகிழ்விழ்ந்தாய் தூளிவணக்கன்டுஞ்சனம   ப்
மினிடுகையினித்தநாமொபொங்கிளரொாழ்துமென்பா   ம்

*If the beauteous flowers, budding like gems, expanding with the bril-
liancy of the stars of heaven, and shedding scented honey in drops like the
whitest pearls, if these fade in a day, and falling torn to the earth crum-
ble into dust, can our bodies, blemished with the disease of birth, live for
ever ?*

Example of a stanza beginning with a long syllable :

அல்கினமாரியஹணயத்றத்திஞ   ன்
சொல்கினமாததினையிற்கடநூர்ப்பஞொர்
கல்கினமாரியகைகவருசதாஎ   அு
வில்கினமாரியினவீ ஈன்விலகஞு   ன்

இராமாயணம - பாலகாணடம - தாடகைவதபபபடலம - எடக- கவி.

Black as the stormy cloud, she sent forth from her hands, a shower of stones such as might fill up the ocean, in the time of the utterance of a word. This he opposed by a shower from his bow.

LXIII. First. The consonance எதுகை was stated to require, that, in each line, the second letter should be of the same class and quantity: I said *letter*, and not syllable; because, in the word கற்பு, for instance, the second syllable is பு, and if I merely retain it, and write தப்பு, or நட்பு, the second letter, ற, is then changed, and the consonance is, therefore, faulty. It would be better to put some word like பற்று, but best of all to use அற்பு, பொற்பு, &c.

Secondly. If the second letter be ய், and be followed by another consonant, in the same syllable, as in the word மெய்ப்பொருள், no notice is then taken of the ய்; but the ப் only is considered: so that, the எதுகை will be perfect, if we have, in the other lines, எப்பொருள, அப்பொருள, &c. But if the ய் be not followed by another consonant, in the same syllable, the எதுகை will not be thought good, unless ய், or at all events, ஐ occur in the following lines; thus, மெய்வகை, பெய்வகை, கைவகை, மைவகை, &c. agree well in consonance; not so the words வாய்வகை, மாவகை, &c.

Thirdly. Instances are to be found, in which the consonants ர், ல், ழ், when they happen to occur in the first syllable, are not taken into account; but it is, nevertheless, improper to overlook them. Thus, கார்த்த is made consonous with பார்த்த, அல்வேறு with பால்வேறு, and மாழ்த with வாழ்நத. The following stanza, therefore, from an ancient poet, is objectionable.

அந்தாத்துள்ளேயகைபுறங்கையா   ம்
அந்தாபெபொதுமவினவாழ்க்கை – அந்தாத   து
வாழினெற்றெனறுமகிழ்தன்மின்வாளுரு   ஊ
போகினறுஉவன்மெயபொன   று

As the palm of the hand may readily be turned outwards in the open air, so quickly mutable is domestic life.—Say not we shall live for a term.—The days of our life are as the flowers of the Púlei. *

---

* Illecebrum Javanicum—of which the soft and downy flowers are scattered by the wind.

The objection to this stanza is, that போகின்ற has been used as an எதுகை to வாழ்கின்ற.

Fourthly, and lastly. In the வெண்பா alone, and in that but seldom, instead of repeating the same letter for the எதுகை, one of the same class only, is used ; that is, a rough letter is made to correspond to a rough letter, and a mediate, to a mediate. Example:

தக்கார் - தகவில் - ஒன்ப - தவரவு

ஒச்சததாற் - காணப் - படு   ம்

திருவ - டெ, அடி - ச, குற.

The worth or demerit (of parents) *is conspicuous in the offspring.*

Here, எச்சததால் is used as an எதுகை to தக்கார் ; that is, ச் is made to correspond to ச்: but this is inelegant.

LXIV. It was stated, that the quantity of the first syllable must be preserved. Remark, however, that. though ஐ and ஒள are long, yet, since they are diphthongs, the first corresponds to அ before the mute consonant ய், and the second to அ before the mute consonant வ்: accordingly, if the first line begin with one of those diphthongs, we must not, in the other lines, use a long letter, but a short one before ய் or வ், as the case may require. Hence, the following words are consonous : கைகவகை, டுமயவகை, டுபாயவகை, &c. as also ஒளவியம, நவவியம, &c.

LXV. It was also stated, that each of the lines in a stanza ought to commence with a different letter. Nevertheless, as some words have various significations, it is esteemed elegant to begin all the lines with the same word, provided it have a different meaning in each line. Example :

கன்னை - டிவருங் - கழுதாரிங் - தமிரு   ங்

கன்னை - டிமயில் - கங்கலா - படமா   டு

கன்னை - டியெழிற் - கனையா - டிடெடுங்

கன்னை - டிகழுங் - கயமா - டினளா ல்

The long-eyed damsel, having chosen a spot where the swarms of humming wasps sought honey, sported with the peacocks on the beautiful banks of the watery mirror (that reflected their) *outspread tails, and then bathed in the sparkling waters of the flowery tank.*

Here, கண்ணுடி occurs four times: in the first line, it is கண்நாடி; in the second, it has the force of இடங்காடி; in the third, it is கண்ணுடி; and in the fourth, கண்ணுடிகெழ். Another Example:

நாக - டெந்றியி - னன்டணி - டயாடைடபா

ஞுக - டெந்றியி - னன்மணி - யாறுயா ய்

நாக - டெந்றியி - னன்மவிர்க் - காவய பா

ஞுக - டெந்றியி - னன்மது - டதானநிறடற

டதமபாவணி - பைதாநீகருபடடம - உஅ, கவி.

(They had now passed) the grove of Nāgas, watered by the stream which flows bearing gems from the mountain top, like the jewel-spangled frontlet that hangs on the forehead of the elephant; and now the waning moon appeared on the verge of the heavens.

In this விருததம், நாகம occurs four times, with different significations. In the first line, it means *an elephant;* in the second, *a mountain;* in the third, *a tree—the calophyllum inophyllum;* in the fourth, *heaven.*

LXVI. Besides எதுகை, of which we have hitherto been speaking, there is another kind of consonance, which the lines in a stanza may have one with another. It is termed இயைபு, and is the rhyme at the close of lines, which is used in the poetry of the languages of Europe. This kind of consonance, however, being despised as wanting in dignity, is hardly to be met with in any species of poetry. There are still other sorts of rhyme, which, as they are very seldom used, I think it unnecessary to explain; but refer the reader, who may wish for information respecting them, to the work intitled காரிகை.

CHAPTER II.

பா

LXVII. A stanza of two, three, or more commonly of four lines, is distinguished in Tamil by the several names of பா, பாடடு, கவி, யாபபு, டசயயுள. Of these, கவி, is the proper name; the rest being tropical designations. The stanza is termed பா *(warp)*, from its regularity; பா

ட்டு (*song*), from its being sung; யாப்பு (*link*), from the connexion of its parts; and செய்யுள், from its measured cadence. The பா is divided into five kinds, வெண்பா, ஆசிரியப்பா, கலிப்பா, வஞ்சிப்பா, மருட்பா. Of the first kind, which is the commonest, the most difficult in its construction, and the most esteemed, I shall treat at large; contenting myself with a brief notice of the rest.

SECTION THE FIRST.
வெண்பா

LXVIII. In this kind of verse are used the feet termed இயற்சீர் and வெஞ்சீர், namely, those of the second and third classes, which have been already described. The stanza, however, must always end with a foot of the first class; nor is it allowable to affix ஏ at its close, as is sometimes done in other kinds of verse. The rules contained in No. LVII, for the connexion termed வெண்டளை, must be strictly observed. In order to explain the number of அடி, or lines required to form one வெண்பா, and the number of feet of which each அடி must consist, it is necessary to premise, that there are six kinds of வெண்பா, namely, குறள்வெண்பா, சிந்தியல்வெண்பா, நேரிசைவெண்பா, *சவலைவெண்பா, இன்னிசைவெண்பா, டம்றுடைவெண்பா. Of these I shall treat separately.

LXIX. First குறள்வெண்பா. This resembles the distich, since it consists of two lines. Of these, the first must contain four feet, and the second three. Example :

கணணுடைய - ரெனபவர் - கற்றோர் - முகத்திரண்டு
புணணுடையர் - கல்லா - தவ   ர்

திருவ - சய், அதி - ௳, குற.

They may be said to have eyes, who acquire knowledge.—They who learn not, have (as it were) *only two ulcers in their face.*

Here the order of the feet is கூவிளைஙகாய, கூவிளம, தேமா, கருவிள ஙகாய, கூவிளைஙகாய, தேமா, மலர். This kind of வெண்பா is sometimes without either of the rhymes எதுகை and மோனை, thus;

---

* This measure is also termed சமனிலை வெண்பா.

சீரின - றமையா - துலெனின் - யார்யார்க்குடி
வானின - றமையா - தொழுக ௫
திருவ - உ, அதி - ய, குற.

*If worldly prosperity be not attainable unless the rain falls, so neither
can its continuance be insured unless the heavens be* (propitious.)

Neither the one nor the other occurs in this stanza. Sometimes, though
rarely, you will find three feet only in the first line, and four in the
second : as,

மனத்துக்கண் - மாசில - ஞ்தி
வெண்ததற - ஞ்குல - நீர - மிற
திருவ - சு, அதி - சு, குற.

*To have the mind pure from spot, that is the standard of virtue—all
besides is* (empty) *sound.*

மனத்தாஞ் - மாநதர்க - ஞனர்ச இ
யினத்தாஞ் - மிஞ - னைனயபடுஞ்-சொல்
திருவ - சய்கா, அதி - ஈ, குற.

*The understanding of a man hath its source in his own mind—his
character among men is determined by his fellowships.*

LXX. Secondly. Passing over சிகதியல்வெனபா, of which I shall
speak last, I proceed to consider செநிசைவெனபா. This is the kind of
வெனபா most in use, so that, by way of eminence, it has been termed
வெனபா, simply. It consists of two குறள்வெனபா, with one detached
foot interposed, which is termed, on that account, தனிசொல். This
must have the same எதுகை as the two first lines. It is followed by two
other lines, either with the same எதுகை, or, what is more general, with
another. If the தனிசொல், be a foot containing only one kind of அசை,
for example, a தேமா, which consists of two நேர், a தேமாஙகாய,
which consists of three நேர், or a கருவினம, which consists of two நிரை,
then the stanza is termed நாஙிடை செநிசை வெனபா: but if it be a foot
containing both kinds of அசை, like the five remaining feet of the second
and third classes, the stanza is then termed ஈராஙிடைசெநிசைவெனபா:
Example.

செய்ய - குறறேறுன றி - வெளுசினவே - றுடகொளி னும் த்
பெய்யு - மழைமூழ்கிஷிப - பேணுவாால - வைய த்
இருளபொழியுவ - குறறத - பல்வெனினும - யார்கரு ம்
பொருளபொழியாா - மெறறே - புக ழ்

As the clouds which send forth a fearful sound, and are big with the angry thunder-bolt, are yet cherished for the rain they pour down ; so in the world, he who liberally distributes his wealth is praised, though his many crimes spread darkness around him.

Here, since வையத் is a தனிசசொல consisting of two நேர், (நேதமா) the stanza is called நாஷிடை நேரிசைவெனபா.

எஞ்சிரு - நிலவல - யெனகடெகேதாா - யினனுயிர்கொ ள்
உஞ்சிரு - எஞ்சாது - போயகல்க - வெஞசமதது ம்
போாதவாாகத் - தனநிப - பிறர்முதுகி ற்
சாாவென - வையிற - சா ம்

Of those who oppose me, none shall retain much-loved life. All who fear may withdraw securely. The arrows of my hand pierce the hearts of those who firmly withstand my valour—they enter not the backs of my enemies.

Here, வெஞசமதது is the foot called கூவிளைஙகாய ; hence the வெணபா is termed னாாஷிடை நேரிசைவெனபா.

LXXI. Thirdly. சயவலவெணபா. This consists of four lines, without the தனிசசொல. The first line contains four feet; the second, three; the third, four; and the fourth, three; all under one எதுகை. The only specimen of this kind of stanza is in the work called மூதுனா, on which account, it has, by some, been termed மூதுனாவெணபா. The stanza is

அடடாலும - பாலசுவையிற - குனறு - தாவல லை
நடடாலும - நணபல்லார் - நணபல்ல க்
கெடடாலும - மேனமகக - மேனமகக - ளேசஙரு
சுடடாலும - வெணமை - தரு ம்

Though milk be boiled, it loseth not it's flavor. Though one void of affection be immeasurably loved, no love is (returned). *The illustrious, though ruined, are still great--the conch tho' burned, gives forth whiteness.*

LXXII. Fourthly. இனவிசைஒெண்பா. This usually consists of four lines, of which, the first three contain each four feet; and the fourth, three feet. They may all come under one எதுகை; or, by couples, under two எதுகை. Example:

இன்றுகோ - லனறுடகா - ெள்னறுகோ - ெலனருது

பின்னைறடேய - நினற்து - கூறற்மென - ற்றன ணீ

ெயாருவுயின் - நீ யவை - ெயால்இம - வகயா ன்

மருவுயின் - மாணடா - ரற ம்

நாலடிநானூறு - அ, எடு - அற்னவயியுறுத்தல் சூ, பா.

Say not to-day, or that day, or any day; but reflect that death is ever standing behind you. Eschew evil, and with unceasing endeavours adhere to virtue, ordained by sages.

Sometimes it consists of lines of the same measure as the above, but without an எதுகை; repeating, at the end of each line, the word with which that line commenced. This variety is termed ஒருஉத்ெதாடை. Example:

மழையினநி - மாகிலத்தார்க - கிலவி - மழையுங்

தவமுஉனா - நில்வழி - யில்லவிஷ்த - தவ மூ

மாசுஉனா - னில்வழி - யில்லஷி - யாச ்து

யில்ஷாமழவா - னில்வழி - யி வ்

நானமணிகடி கை - சு அ, பா.

If rain fail the inhabitants of the earth suffer: where no penitents are found, the rain falls not; penitence is not performed where there is no king, and kings reign not where civil society does not exist.

It may also, like the second kind of ெவண்பா, consist of one line of four feet, one of three, and a தனிச்ெசால்; all having one எதுகை; then a line of four feet, and one of three, without any எதுகை, thus:

ெபாொள் - ேவணடி ற - ெபாருள்ெபாழ்க - பினறகைேத

ெசாப - ெபாருெஎணடி ற - நீெதாருிக - பாருஷிேம ன

மனினபம - ேவணடினறம - வாய்க்க - துயின மை

ேவணடின - ெவகுஷி - விட வ்

If thou covetest fame, distribute riches. If thou desirest the riches which follow a man into future existence, flee from sin in this world. If thou wishest the highest and most permanent delight, practise virtue. If thou wouldest be free from sorrow, repress anger.

Lastly. It may have the first line of four feet, the second of three, the third of four, then a தனிசொல; after which, follows the fourth line, of three feet; all comprised under two எதுகை. Example:

நீலரு - சுவணததன்ன - தீர்மை - தயைகிவிஞ்த	தே
ஞாலக - தரிமென்றுமை - நடபிலலார் - பூமணமூ	ம
பூடேளனியும - பொனறு - மணிெயாவிபு - மாமன்	ரு
காமணடநத - சீர்கெலலா - நட	பு

As the nymphœa inhabits the water-springs, so dwells philanthropy in (the heart of) the benevolent. If they who are devoid of love should give the whole earth, what avails it? As sweet odours grace the flower, as the spark of brilliancy glitters in the splendid jewels and never-fading gems, so is love the grace of all our virtues.

Of these four varieties of இனனிசைெவணபா, you will sometimes meet with the first, but hardly ever with the others.

LXXIII. Fifthly. பஃெறுடைெவணபா. This contains more than four lines, (அடி) having five, six, or even a greater number. Of these, the last must always have three feet, and the rest four; the whole under one, two, or more எதுகை. Scarcely a single example of this kind of ெவண பா, is to be found.

LXXIV. Sixthly. நெதியலெவணபா. This consists of three lines. It may either, like நேரிசைெவணபா, have under one எதுகை, the first line of four feet, the second of three, and a தனிெசால; these being followed by a line of three feet, under another எதுகை, in which case, it is called நேரிசைசநெதியலெவணபா: Or, like இனனிசைெவணபா, it may have two lines of four feet and one of three, without a தனிெசால; and coming either under one எதுகை, or under two: or, instead of this, each line may have the ஒருஉததெதாடை already described. In either case, it is termed இனனிசைசசநெதியலெவணபா. The நெதியலெவணபா, like the பஃெறு

றடஒெனபா, is very little used. I shall, therefore, content myself with giving an example of the variety termed ஞேசிௗசசஇஈஙஙிபல.

ஆனிஎறமஓெவ - ருஷிஇு - மஈஙிஎறதத - வாஈபயஈத
பாணிஎறமஓெவ - றலல - பலகுலதஓெதா
ஈாஎஙிஷியின

ஓெவஒஈறனி ஐுஞு - செயயஈறஓெஞு - ஓெய

Tho' the colour of cows be various, yet the milk they yield differs not in colour : tho' nations be many and of various habits, is the virtue they practice essentially various?

LXXV. Thus much of the ஒெனபா; a kind of verse which the natives consider so difficult, that they have named it *the tiger of poets*. At the present day, very few can be found sufficiently skilled in the rules relating to it, even to scan a ஒெனபா ; much less to compose one : although, by us, the difficulty may be overcome by the study of a single hour.

It is to be remarked that, in the ஒெனபா, not only are all the rules which have been laid down respecting it's metre to be strictly observed ; but a more than ordinary attention must be paid to elegance and conciseness in the diction. The thoughts should, in the style of the epigram, be pointed ; and ought to be so artfully involved, that, although the meaning of the individual words be known, there should still remain something to be discovered. I shall give an example ; not perhaps, the best that might be adduced, but the first which presents itself : it is a குஐ எஒெவெனபா, from the poet இருவளஙருவன.

உருவுஈணெ - மௌடஎனளஈணைம - ஓெவெணஇு - முருஎஒெபருஈஓெதிர்ஈ
ஈசசஈஙி - யஎனஞு - ருைஎடஈத
ஈூஙெ - அஇ - எ, குஐ.

Which may be literally translated thus : *Despise not a man on account of his appearance ; for there are some who may be compared to the linch pin in the axletree of a mighty car :* i. e. there are persons who, though mean in their appearance, are yet useful and necessary to the state ; just as the linch pin of the axletree, though rudely formed, is yet highly useful, and a necessary appendage to the carriage. If this pointed turn be wanting, the ஒெனபா should, at least, have something striking in the sentiment: like the following instance, taken also from Tiruvalluver:

அறத்தினூஉங் - காக்கமு - மில்லை - யதனை
மறத்தலி - னூஉங்கில்லை - கே டு

௪, அதி - ௨, ௩௨.

There is no profit greater than virtue, and no loss greater than is sustained by forsaking it.

SECTION THE SECOND.

ஆசிரியப்பா.

LXXVI. This kind of verse, which is also called அகவல், admits, properly, the feet of the second class, termed இயற்சீர்; and the connexion called ஆசிரியத்தளை. Besides the feet peculiar to it, it admits those of the third class, வெண்சீர்; and, occasionally, of the fourth class, the two kinds, தேமாங்கனி and புளிமாங்கனி; and besides the connexion proper to it, it admits those termed வெண்டளை and வஞ்சித்தளை. The number of lines, or அடி, in each stanza, is not defined; nor is there any settled rule for the number of feet requisite to each line. Observe, however:

First. That if, while the other அடி consist of four feet, the last but one consists of three only, the stanza is called நேரிசையாசிரியப்பா.

Secondly. That if the first and last அடி consist of four feet, and the intermediate lines consist, by pairs, of two or of three feet, the stanza is termed இணைக்குறளாசிரியப்பா.

Thirdly. That if all the lines consist of four feet, the stanza is called நிலைமண்டிலவாசிரியப்பா.

Fourthly. That if, not only all the lines agree in the number of their feet, but the matter be so arranged, that they may be transposed at pleasure, and still preserve the metre and the sense entire; the stanza is then called அடிமறிமண்டிலவாசிரியப்பா. I subjoin an example of the last mentioned kind:

ஞால் - பரவிய - திருகோன் - யாறே
ஞா - மகளி - ராரணை - கின தோ

வார- ெலினிேல-யானைரு-கவேில

சார-ஞட-ீயர-ெ   ேற

Oh thou who dwellest on the mountain's side, come not by the road where the tangled rattan skirts the silvan stream, and where the nymphs (who devise) mischief and inflict evil abound. *I dread thy journeying on that road.*

Finally. The author of Càrigei remarks, that, in this kind of verse, எ may be added, with excellent effect, at the close of the stanza.

SECTION THE THIRD.

கலிப்பா.

LXXVII. This kind of verse admits two feet of the class இயற்சீர், namely, கருவிளாம, கூவிளம ; all the feet of the class ெயச்சீர், especially those which begin with a நிளா ; and, of the class வஞ்சிச்சீர், the feet termed ேதமாஙகஸி and புளிமாஙகஸி. Besides the connexion கஷிததஷெ, which is proper to it, it admits also those called ஆஷியததஷ and ெவ ஷைடஷெ. It consists of four lines, of four feet each. Example:

ெசல்வபேபார்க-கதக்கணைன - ெசயிர்ததெதறிநத- இனவா ஷி

மூல்வஷிததார்- மறமனைர்- முடிடசதவிலைய- முருகஷெப   ேபா

ெயல்வஷதீர்- வியனெகாணமூ- விடைநஷைமுயு - மஷியமேபாா் ஷ்

மல்லேலாஙம- ெகஷில்யாவஷை - மருமம்பாய்ங்- ெதாளிதத   ேத

The keen Chacram furiously thrown by the angry eyed warrior after severing the crowned heads of heroic kings decked with jasmin wreaths, sunk and disappeared in the forehead of the powerful and mighty elephant, like the moon entering a dense immeasurable cloud.

The work intitled Càrigei describes many varieties of this metre; which, as they are now almost obsolete, I do not think it necessary to mention; but refer the reader to that treatise, for information on the subject.

SECTION THE FOURTH.

வருசிப்பா.

LXXVIII. This metre, besides the feet which are proper to it, viz. those of the class வருசிசசீர், admits all the other classes; and though the mode of connexion proper to it, is that termed வருசிததளை, it admits also all the other modes already described. The stanza may contain any number of lines, not less than three; and these must be either குறளடி., lines of two feet, or சிந்தடி, lines of three feet. As this kind of verse is now hardly known, even by name, it is unnecessary to say more respecting it.

SECTION THE FIFTH.

மருட்பா.

LXXIX. The term மருட்பா is derived from the word மருள், signifying *confusion*, because, in this kind of verse, the வெணபா and the ஆசிய ப்பா are intermixed. The stanza begins with two lines of the measure வெணபா, and the remainder is of the measure ஆசியப்பா, of which the number of lines is not limited. This metre is very little used, and, unlike the other kinds, has not those subdivisions of which I proceed to treat.

CHAPTER III.

இனம்.

LXXX. The word இனம் means *consanguinity*, and is used to express those kinds of verse which, being subdivisions of the foregoing, may, therefore, be said to bear a sort of relationship to them. These subdivisions are three, தாழிசை, துறை, விருததம், which, according to their application to the several kinds of verse, are termed as follows:

வெண்டாழிசை - வெண்டுறை - வெளிவிருதத   ம்
ஆசிரியத்தாழிசை - ஆசிரியததுறை - ஆசிரியவிருததம்
கலித்தாழிசை - கலிததுறை - கலிவிருதத   ம்
வஞ்சித்தாழிசை - வஞுசிததுறை - வஞுசிவிருதத   ம்

I propose to treat of these subdivisions in the present chapter.

SECTION THE FIRST.

தாழிசை.

LXXXI. A succession of three stanzas, of any kind, each of which has its several lines ending with the same word (*) as the corresponding lines of the others, is usually termed தாழிசை.

First. A succession of three similar stanzas, each of which contains three lines, equal in the number of their feet, and terminating, respectively, with the same word as the corresponding lines of the other stanzas, is called ஆசிரியததாழிசை. Example:

பாமபு - கயிறுக - கடல்கடைநத - மாமாய   ன்
நாங்குநம - மாறுள் - வருதே - லவனவாசி   ன்
ஆமபல்ந - தீவகுழல் - கேளா - மோரதா   ழி

கொலைளியநு - சாரற் - குருநதாசிதத - மாமையன்
எலதிநம - மாறுள் - வருதம - லவனவாயி   ன்
முலையந - தீவகுழல் - கேளா - மோரதா   ழி

கனறு - குளிலாக - கவியுகுதத - பாமாய   ன்
இனறுநம - டாறுள் - வருதே - லவனவாயி   ற்
கொளைரயந - தீகுழல் - கேளா - போரதா   ழி
செயபததாரம - இததாவிழ - காதை - ஆசி யர்குரைவ.

If the mighty Màyen (Vishnu) who churned the ocean, using the snake as his churning rope, should come hither amidst our herds, shall we not hear the sweet àmbel pipe sounded by his mouth, O my friend?

(*) This correspondence in the terminations of the lines is not indispensable. No mention is made of it in Càrigei; and Beschi himself, in his Tonnùl Vilacam states it to be optional. See the fifth line in each of the examples quoted in No. LVI. and No. LVII.

If the mighty Màyen who tore down the (false) *Curundu tree in the field near our garden, should come among our herds, while the sun is up, shall we not hear the sweet mullei pipe sounded by his mouth, O my friend?*

If the great Màyen who whirling the young calves as sticks, knocked down with them the fruits (from the trees) *should this day come hither amidst our herds, shall we not hear the sweet condei pipe sounded by his mouth, O my friend?*

LXXXII.   Secondly.   A succession of three similar stanzas, each of two lines, of which the second contains a greater number of feet than the first, and having the several lines of each stanza ending with the same word as the corresponding lines of the others, is termed கவி தத்தாழி சை. Example:

ெகாயஇவஊக - காததுஊ - குளவி - யஇுகக்தஇெத	ம்
ெபாயதற் - சி றுகுடில - வாரனீ - ையயங லமஉவணடி ன்	
ஆயஇவஊக - காதது - மருவி - யஇுகக்தஇெத	ம்
மாயதற் - சி றுகுடில - வாரனீ - ையயகல்ம உவணடி ன்	
ெமன நிஇவஊக - காதது - மிகுழுக - கமழுசா	வஇ
குனநிற் - சி றுகுடில - வாரனீ - ையயநலமஉவணடி ன்	

We watch the reaping of the Tineinear the verdant hill. If you would be happy with us, come not, O Sir, to our crowded cottage.

We watch the winnowing of the Tinei, near the vernal hill. If you would be happy with us, come not, O Sir, to our sheltered cottage.

We watch the tender Tinei on the hills where the groves abound with scented flowers. If you would be happy with us, come not, O Sir, to our humble cottage.

LXXXIII.   Thirdly.   A succession of three similar stanzas, each with four lines of two feet, and having the several lines of each stanza ending with the same word as the corresponding lines of the others, is called வருசிததாழிசை. Example:

மடடயிடிஐயு - மதடேவுழ   ங
தடகையால் - ஒவயின்மைறகூகு ம்
இடைசசர - பிறநதார்க   டே
நடகுமென் - மன்டேனகா   என்

டேடையே - யிருமடோாததது   த்
டோைஐயால் - ஒவயின்மைறகூகு   ங்
காடட - பிறநதார்க   டே
டேடுமை - பன்டேனகா   என்

இருமபிடிஐயை - யிகலடேவுழ ம்
பெருஙைஐயால் - ஒவயினமைணறகூகும்
அருஞுசர - பிறநதார்க   டே
விருமபுமெள் - பன்டேனகா   என்

My thoughts go along with him who is journeying through the fiery desert, where the male elephant with his long proboscis shades the gentle females from the burning sun.

My thoughts seek him who is journeying in the wilderness, where the peacock with his outspread tail shades the pea-hen from the burning sun.

My thoughts long for him who is journeying through the burning desert, where the mighty male elephant with his great proboscis shades the gentle females from the burning sun.

LXXXIV. Fourthly. The தாழிசை which is formed from the வெணபா, and which is termed வெணடாழிசை, or வெணடொாததாழிசை, is a single stanza. Like the செிதியலவெணபா, it has the two first lines of four feet, and the third of three. It ends like the வெணபா, but does not conform to the connexion வெணடளை. Example:

நணபி - ஒதனறு - தீய - ஒசால்லார்
முனபு - ஙினறு - முளிவு - ஒசயயார்
அனபு - ஒவணடு - பவ   ர்

They who desire affection will speak no ill, nor stand in angry opposition : this they will consider real friendship.

Besides these varieties of தாழிசை, others, for each kind of verse, are enumerated in the work called Càrigei, but as they are all very little employed, it would be loading the subject with useless matter, to describe them, at the present day. The name and cadence of the தாழிசை are sometimes applied to a kind of metre, of which the proper appellation is கழிநெடிலடிவிருத்தம், and of which I shall presently treat.

———•◦◅◖◗▻◦•———

SECTION THE SECOND.

துறை.

LXXXV. Of this kind of metre, the variety termed கவிததுறை is the only one which is much used and esteemed ; to it, therefore, I shall confine my remarks. This kind of stanza consists of four lines, under one எதுகை ; and always takes எ at it's close. Each line has five feet, of which the first four must be among these six, தேமா, புளிமா, கருவிளம், கூவிளம், தேமாங்காய், புளிமாங்காய். The fifth foot should invariably be either a கருவிளங்காய், or a கூவிளங்காய். On this foot, the consonance மோனை ought to fall ; and this is indispensable to the beauty of the line, even though there be a மோனை or some other foot. The connexion of the feet can only be that termed வெண்டளை ; which, however, does not here, as it invariably must with the வெண்பா, affect the commencement of one line with reference to the ending of that which precedes it ; but only regards each, individually considered : thence, although the lines in this metre must end in a காய், they need not therefore commence with a நேரசை.

This metre is distinguished into two varieties, depending on the number of syllables in the line. If the stanza begin with a syllable, long either by nature or by prosody, each அடி will contain sixteen syllables ; and the stanza is termed நேரசைகவிததுறை. If the stanza begin with a short syllable, each அடி will contain seventeen syllables, and the stanza is then termed நிரையசைகவிததுறை. These two varieties are commonly termed நேர்பதினாறு and நிரைபதினேழு. If the line contain only the feet abovementioned, and the வெண்டளை be observed, it will necessarily consist of one or other of these two numbers of syllables. The கவிதத்துறை, then, like the வெண்பா, admits of no deviation from the rules prescribed for it's construction: both these kinds of. metre are, therefore, difficult ; but they are held in proportionate esteem. I subjoin, by way of example, a கிளையசைகவிதத்துறை, that is, one of seventeen syllables, in which I have comprised all the foregoing rules:

இடையேயுடநர்- வெணசீ - நியநசீர் - வருமுத - சீரிருசீ   ர்
கடடேய - யிடடகினா - வெணசீராய - வெணடவிக - காததடடிநான்
குடடேய - கடடயாயக - கடடேமாவண - நானகடடி - யோமொதுகை
நடடேய- கவிததுறை - யாமெனக - கறடேரா- நவினதன   சே
தானநூலவிளககம - யாபபதிகாரம - உரைசயக, ரூத.

In the treatise entitled Càrigei, the term கவிததுறை is also applied to a stanza consisting of four lines, which are under one எதுகை, and are similarly constructed செடடிஅடி, that is, lines of five feet. It is now confounded with the விருததம. Example:

ஒனறு - ரருசும - வணசிவிகி -யருசா - வரிநனனூ   ற்
சொனனர் - சொலலிலும - பாவரை - யருசாச - சுடரமொயபப
மினறர் - மனனர் - கோடடொளாவி - யருசா - விநியாப   டு
வனனர் - சேடடரு - சாவிலி - வெனனறு - வறியாரயா   ர்
தமபாவணீ - முடிருடடுபபடடலம - எயூடு, கவி.

Who is ignorant that death fears not the strong bow dreaded by enemies,---nor the works in verse or prose of such as have made all learning their own,---nor the splendour of the king's sceptre, sparkling with innumerable refulgent rays,---nor the beauty of such as resemble the unexpanded flower?

For the sake of distinction, this kind of stanza is called காபபியகவிததுறை ; while that of which we first spoke, is termed கடடவிகவிததுறை, or simply கவிததுறை.

SECTION THE THIRD.
விருததம.

LXXXVI. The விருததம is the metre in which all the great poetical narrations are composed ; and it is, therefore, more extensively used than any other. It is distinguished into several kinds, all which contain four அடி, or lines, under one எதுகை. If each line is of three feet, the stanza is termed வஞ்சிவிருத்தம ; if of four, கவிவிருத்தம; if of four, with a தனிச்சொல் after each line, வெளிவிருத்தம ; if of more than five feet, as six, seven, or a greater number, ஆசிரியவிருத்தம. These terms are not now in use, but the several species of stanza are named from the length of the அடி (see No. LX.) which compose them. Thus, if the lines consist of two feet, the stanza is superscribed குறளடிவிருத்தம ; if of three, சிந்தடிவிருத்தம ; if of four, அளவடிவிருத்தம ; if of five, நெடிலடி விருத்தம; if of more than five, கழிநெடிலடிவிருத்தம.

LXXXVII. The விருத்தம admits all kinds of feet; but those of the fifth class, போதுச்சீர், (see No. LIV.) are very seldom used. The இயற்சீர், வெண்சீர், and வஞ்சிச்சீர், and, of the last mentioned class, those especially which end in விளங்கனி, are the feet most commonly employed: This kind of verse has no தளை, or connexion of feet, appropriated to it: we are merely told, that the stanza should always contain four lines, equal both in the number of their feet, and in metre. In what this equality of metre consists, I have not been able to ascertain from any author ; nor were any of the learned whom I consulted, able to inform me : for they themselves do not read their verses, but repeat them in a kind of recitative; so that, according to their account, they perceived this equality of the metre by their ear, a mode which appeared to me difficult for foreigners, and too unscientific for so elegant an art as poetry. Thus much, however, I remarked, that, in the விருத்தம, none of the rules for connexion were regularly observed: for instance, a foot ending in a சேர் was followed, indiscriminately, either by a சேர் or a நிரை ; so also with a நிரை : and, in the same stanza, one line would have a நிரையசை, where another had a சேரசை, and contrariwise; notwithstanding which, the lines corresponded in cadence. Yet, if I myself connected the different feet together as I chose, only preserving the proper number, the line was lame, and out of time. I remarked further, not only that stanzas which were exactly equal in the number of their feet, were different in their cadence, but that the change was marked in their books by the word வேறு, *different*: the words சந்தம், or வண்ணம், which signify *cadence*, being understood. The different kinds of விருத்தம் which may be obtained by diversifying the cadence, are so numerous, that the poet கம்பன் has introduced, in his Ràmàyanam, no less than eighty-seven varieties; although, in the construction of his stanzas, he has, for the most part, confined himself to lines of four, five, or six feet. After considerable pains and study, I at length succeeded in discovering the cause of this diversity.

LXXXVIII. The varieties of cadence do not depend exclusively, either on the number of feet in the line, or on their connexion (தளை) ; but on the diversity of the feet themselves. In order to explain this, it becomes necessary to class the feet in a different order from that observed in chapter I. Omitting, then, the sixteen feet termed பொதுச்சீர், since they are rarely used, the rest may be arranged as follows :

The first class consists of the feet which end in மா, தேமா, புளிமா,

The second, of those which end in விளம்; கருவிளம், கூவிளம்,

The third, of those which end in காய்; தேமாங்காய், &c.

The fourth, of those ending in மாங்கனி; தேமாங்கனி, புளிமாங்கனி.

The fifth, of those ending in விளங்கனி; கருவிளங்கனி, கூவிளங்கனி.

From the various ways in which these five kinds of feet are connected, arise the several varieties of cadence, and as the mode of connexion may be constantly altered, the changes of cadence, or சந்தம், will be proportionably numerous. For instance, in the அளவடிவிருத்தம், each line of which contains four feet, if you use only the two kinds of மா, and of விளம், you may connect them in fourteen different ways; thereby producing an equal number of cadences: some of them, however, will not be very pleasing to the ear. Again, in the கழிவிருத்தம், the lines of which contain each five feet, these two kinds of feet may be arranged in thirty different ways; and so on, according to the number of feet employed. On this principle, it is so easy to invent new சந்தம், that, whilst those who are unacquainted with it, applaud the poet Camben, because, in his Ràmàyanam, which contains 12,016 stanzas, he has introduced

87 varieties of cadence, I, in my poem Témbàvani, which contains only 3,615 stanzas, have, without any difficulty, made 90 variations. It would, indeed, have been easy to give a different cadence to every stanza; but this could not have been done with propriety, as the same cadence is usually preserved through ten, fifteen, or more stanzas.

LXXXIX. With these introductory remarks, I proceed to lay down the following rules:

Rule 1st. After the first line of the stanza is composed, the same class of feet, and the same arrangement of them must be preserved in the other three; so that, if, in the first line, we have மா, in the corresponding place, in the other lines, we cannot use விளம, nor காய், nor கவி, but only மா: and so of any other foot. To this rule there is no exception.

XC. Rule 2d. Feet of the same class may, in general, be interchanged, without affecting the cadence; so that, if, in one line, we have தேமா, we may use புளிமா in the corresponding place in any other line of the same cadence, even though it be in the same stanza. In like manner, கூவிளம may be used to correspond to கருவிளம, &c. This rule applies invariably to the four feet of the third class, வெண்சீர். In the other classes, there are exceptions, as I shall hereafter explain. In the mean time, the following example will serve to illustrate the two rules already laid down.

சிறைபடி - தெரினன் - நீய்ப்பெய் - விலகின ன்
மிறைபடி - முடியின்ன் - டெயர்செய் - வானையன்
எறைபடி-தொடையயின்ன் - னவிபன் - மனனவ ர்
இறைபடி -.தாளின்ன் -ஒருநதன - ஒறஞுஞு ன்
தேமபாவணி- சோசுவனஒெற நிபபட்ட-லம - ஈஉ0க, கவி.

On that day (Adoni-Zedec) the lord of the winged chariot, the warrior whose bow scattered fire, the crescent crowned monarch, the renowned conqueror decked with garlands of everlasting perfume, at whose feet bowed innumerable tributary kings, was sore vexed, and brought low.

The first line of this விருத்தம contains four feet, in the following order: விளம, விளம, மா, விளம; and this order is exactly adhered to in the remaining lines. For, passing over the first foot, which, on account of the எ.துகை, cannot be changed, we find, that the second foot in the first and fourth lines is கூ.விளைம ; and in the second and third, கருவி ளைம; and that the third foot in the first and fourth lines is தேமா, and in the second and third புளிமா. As the corresponding feet, throughout, though not exactly the same, are of the same class, the cadence remains unaltered. I subjoin an example, in which feet ending in காய் are used:

வேலேனர்-கிறுவி-வேசரிரோர்-விரிநது-இவாதத-மயிர்சசெயியா
னூரன-ொாழுகிப-பிணகருபடை-புதடு-நாறும-பெழ்வாயான்
காேனர்-நெருஙகித-தெங்கியல்ரேர்-கழநீன-இவநத-தாடியிரூன்
றூன-நிலமா-சொாருங்கவணதததுஙு-தாங்கும்-குாகு-முகவடிவான்
தேமபாவுணி-குஜுஙகுமநதிாபபடம-எ, கவி.

Like a spear erect stood the ape-faced (demon) *with hair-filled ears broad as those of an ass, with open mouth fetid from the lumps of carrion that dropped from his lips, with a long and red beard close-tangled like the forest underwood, and stiff as the leaves of the coco-palm, himself a matchless mass of impurity.*

This விருததம contains six feet, in the following order; மா, மா, காய், மா, மா, காய். The second foot in each line is புளிமா; the third foot in the first and third lines is கூ விளைஙகாய; in the second, புளிமாஙகாய; and in the fourth, கருவிளைஙகாய; the fourth foot in the fourth line is தேமா; in the other lines, புளிமா; the fifth foot in the second line is தேமா; and in the rest, புளிமா: lastly, the sixth foot in the first and fourth lines is கருவிளைஙகாய, in the second line, தேமாஙகாய; and in the third line கூ விளைஙகாய. Here, according to the foregoing rules, four varieties of feet ending in காய் have been used promiscuously, without affecting the cadence of the stanza.

XCI. Observe, First. In this kind of verse, a certain license is allowed in the measure of the feet: a syllable short by nature, which, coming before a double consonant, is, therefore, long by prosody, may still be joined with another syllable, to form a கிளையசை. Thus, in the first விரு ததம of the two just quoted, instead of இளைபஇ, we might substitute இளைறொகாணட or இளைறயுறற, without altering the cadence. But a syllable longer by nature, can never be considered as short; so that, we cannot substitute a காய் for a விளம், as இறையார்ந்த for இறைபதி. It may be observed, that, if this were done, the two feet would not be of the same class; and the cadence would, consequently be destroyed.

XCII. Secondly. In rule the 2d (XC.) it was stated, that, although the corresponding feet in the different lines of a விருத்தம் need not, in general, be exactly the same, it was, nevertheless, requisite that they should be of the same class. There is, however, a variety of this metre, called *harmonic*, in which, the species of feet is altogether disregarded, and a certain musical flow, termed குதிப்பு, is alone considered. The following is an example:

அடியுடன்றபரி - பரியுடன்றகரி - கரியுடன்ற - தோடியயிபுடேத ர்
மணியுடன்றத்து - தடுயுடன்றகவண - கவணயுடன்ற - கறைமகிதர ப்
மிசியுடன்றவம - சமருடன்றவுட - இடஇடன்ற - வுயிர்பிரிதா ப்
பணியுடன்றருய - வுயருடன்றபடை - படயுடன்ற - மறையாசருல்
தெம்பாவணி - சோசுவனெடெற றியபடல்ல, கூய்க்கவி.

The horses chafed on their bits —The elephants were rendered impe-tuous by the horses—The cars decked with flags were violently propel-led by the elephants—The bows tinkled with their bells—The arrows were shot forth from the bows—The blood gushed from the arrow wounds—The battle fiercely raged—The bodies were sore-smitten in the battle,—The souls separated and fled from the bodies—thus the pious chief (Joshua) high raised on his jewel-decked chariot, vanquished the opposing hosts.

Here, no regard has been paid to the species of feet employed, but only to the குதிப்பு ; of which, the variety used in this stanza, is exhibited in the following formule : (*)

தனதனந்ததன தனதனந்ததன = தனதனதந்ததன - தன தரு.

In this kind of metre, care must be taken, that the corresponding letters in each line be of the same class ; for if, where in one line there is a soft consonant, we were to employ, in another either a mediate or a rough letter, or a syllable long by nature, although the prosody might not be

---

(*) The several varieties of குதிப்பு are, like the different kinds of feet, expressed by certain formule, in which the metre of each is exhibited.

affected, the harmony would evidently be destroyed. There is no defined limit to the number of these குறிப்பு, that may be interspersed through a poem ; but every one must use his own judgment in introducing them only where they will have a good effect. In the poem Bàradam, they abound even to a disgusting degree. The author appears to have exhausted his labor in the search for words adapted to the harmony, and to have paid no regard to the selection of his thoughts and expressions. Indeed, a person who makes frequent use of harmonic verses, must necessarily sacrifice the sense to the sound. It is best, therefore, to introduce them sparingly, and merely for the purpose of embellishing a subject which seems to require a musical versification. Camben, we see, has done this in his Ràmàyanam, and in Chintàmani this kind of verse does not occur on more than one or two occasions.

XCIII. Thirdly. There is another kind of விருத்தம் termed *semi-harmonic,* in which it is enough, if, where a long syllable occurs in the first line, the corresponding syllables in the other lines be also long, either by nature or position ; nor is it material to what classes the corresponding consonants belong. Moreover, the first foot may begin either with a சேரசை or a நிளையசை. Example :

காரடைந்துளி - வாவியைக் - காத்தபு   ள்
நீரகன்றுயர் - நிற்பது் - காண்பை   ோா
சீரடைந்துளி - மானிடர்-இசெய்யற   ஞ்
ருரைடந்துளி - தொடொ.னாடு - மாற்றுவா   ர்
இதமபாவணி - குணுகுமநிறாப்படலம், ஈம - கவி.

Shall the bird that frequents the replenished pool, be found on it's banks when the water is gone? Man assailed by adversity will exchange for sin the virtues which he practised in prosperity.

In this stanza, it appears, that the succession of long and short syllables is alone observed, and that the corresponding letters are of different classes. The cadence too, would have been the same, if the lines had commenced with a நிளையசை, as முகிளைடந்துளி, &c. This is the metre in which, as was stated in No. LV, the words may be divided, in order to form feet; as is shewn in the foregoing instance.

XCIV. Fourthly. There is another kind of விருத்தம், in which a still smaller degree of harmony is required. In this, it is only necessary, that the harmony should fall on particular feet: thus, in the விருத்தம் already quoted (*) (இகறயஇ &c.) the third foot in each line is a மா, and, as we there explained, might be either a புளிமா or a தேமா: but as the final syllable of that foot, in the first line, is long by position, it cannot, consistently with the harmony, be long by nature in any of the other lines. Again, the fourth foot is a கூவிளம்; and we cannot, therefore, so long as we would preserve this harmony, employ a கருவிளம் in the fourth foot of any of the other lines; although, as in the stanza referred to, we may use it in other feet. Thus, also, in the விருத்தம் cited in No. LXII:

(மகளிபுகா-யருமலி வானஃன-அடிடொவாந்-மலாந்த-தெவணருத்த-தளிபுகா&c.) the harmony falls on the third and sixth feet, which are தேமா; and for which, therefore, புளிமா cannot be substituted: but in the second and fifth feet புளிமா and தேமா will equally suit the cadence. I think it unnecessary to dwell longer on this subject, as a little practice will render it familiar.

XCV. Fifthly. In the celebrated poem Chintàmani, I met with a singular kind of விருத்தம், of which several persons, well skilled in verse, endeavoured to discover the proper cadence, but without success: for the lines, or அடி, were not similarly constructed; and (contrary to a rule lately given,) (†) where, in one line, there was a மா, for instance, in another there would be a விளம், or a காய்; and vice versa. At length I perceived that the விருத்தம் was composed in strict conformity to the connexion வெண்டளை. I proposed, therefore, that it should be recited as a வெண்பா, and we found this to be the proper cadence. I subjoin an example taken from Chintàmani.

மெஉகோத-வணைணன-விளாத்திம்பும்-பும்பிண்டி த்
தெஉகோத-முக்குடை க்ஃழத்-தெஉர்-பெருமாவண

(*) In No. XC.
(†) See No. LXXXIX.

தேவர் - ஒபருமாவிணத் - தெதளுர் - மலிர்சித   றி
நாவி - ன்விற்றுதார் - விட்டுலக - நன்ணு   தே
தேமசியாநிலம்பகம் - ருப் சு, கவி.

They who fail to strew mellifluous flowers before the chief of gods, whose hue is of the swelling ocean, who rests beneath the triple canopy under the odorous blossoming Pindi, they who praise not with their tongue the chief of gods, will ne'er attain the seat of bliss.

Here the first foot in the first and second lines is a தேமாங்காய, and in the third and fourth lines a தேமா ; the second foot in the first line is a தேமா, and in the other lines a காய் ; the third foot in the first and fourth lines is a காய், and in the second and third lines a தேமா ; lastly, the fourth foot in each line is a காய். It will also be seen that the வெண் டளை, or connexion, proper to the verse வெண்பா has been here employed.

In this stanza, the two first lines come under one எதுகை ; after which, the last half of the second line is repeated in the beginning of the third ; and this, with the fourth, comes under another எதுகை. This mode is also used, though rarely, in other kinds of விருத்தம், as has been done in the one quoted in No. XC. beginning அடல்வண்ண, &c. (*). The singular kind of விருத்தம் of which we are now speaking, ought to be very sparingly employed. I have never met with it but in the Chintâmani, the author of which uses it but three times, and then only when he introduces some one singing the praises of the Deity : on no one of these occasions has he exceeded the number of three விருத்தம்.

XCVI. In the poem Bàradam, I have met with another kind of விருத்தம், in which the எதுகை occurring in the beginning of each of the four

(*) This stanza is not to be found in No. XC, nor in any other part of this work. It occurs in Tèmbávani.

அடல்வண்ணத் - தருள்ஒவள்ள - மார்ந்தொதாழக - மல்சியெழுங்
கடல்வண்ணத் - தெவ்வழிருக - தெற்றறருங் - காவை   தே
தெற்றறருங் - காவலெச் - சேர்ஈசவிர்தன - கமல்த்   தா
தொற்றறருஞ் - இநதையய - நிகழ்ழிவு - நன்று   தே
கருவிஷாயனமாட்சிப்பலடம - நாடசு, கவி.

lmes is repeated in the middle, where we should otherwise have the
போன ; so that, instead of four எதுகை, the stanza contains eight.
Example :

வெகுகஇனா - புணட்டமதுப - பஙகயமூ - ஷீலமிர   எ
டஙகலிர்ந்த - தொதத்தல்ரு - மவுகைகுமுக்த - தொாரிருக கை
பைகுகுவளிர - தமணமயிரு - செகுகமலவ - தொாய்தெனவீ
ரஙகையொாடு - கைஜட்ட்ட விி - நகைகயூ - இனறன   தென

*Two eyes bloom in woman's face like two Nilams budding in a lotus
that absorbs the burning sun beams.   The woman wept, and wiping her
eyes with her hands, it seemed as though two red lotus flowers were
plucking two tender Nilams.*

SECTION THE FOURTH.
APPENDIX.

XCVII.   In treating of Tamil metre, I have hitherto considered lines
with regard, as well to their internal structure, as to the mode in which
they are combined in stanzas; and have explained the connexion and
the consonance which they require. I shall now say something regarding
the consonance of one stanza with another.

A stanza, or செயயுள, when it is detached, like our epigram, is termed முத்தகச்செயயுள.   But if several stanzas are connected in a series,
either from their treating of one subject, or from their being the work
of one author, like the epigrams of Martial with us, and the Cural of
Tiruvalluvan in Tamil, the poem is termed தொாகைகிஹிச்சசெயயுள.   If
several stanzas, or distichs, describe one entire action, the poem is called
குஈகசசெயயுள.   Lastly, if, as in the epic poem, &c. they describe
several actions, connected by unity of subject, the poem is termed தொ
டர்ந்ஹிச்சசெயயுள.

XCVIII.   Of the last mentioned kind, there is a subdivision called
தொாறறடெருடா்ந்கிஹிச்சசெயயுள.   It consists of stanzas so connected with
each other, that the following one commences with the same syllable,

word, or words, with which the preceding ended.   Hence, this kind of consonance is termed அந்தாதி, which means *from the end the beginning;* and it is not unfrequently employed, in the several varieties of வெண்பா, கலித்துறை, விருததம், &c., to assist the memory.   Example, from the work called Venbápáttiyel.

மதிகொளட - முககுடைகீழ - வாமன - மலிந்த   தா
இதிதொணந் - நாருந - தொாநூது - நுதிகொள   ட
பல்கதிறேவ - இன்கணளுய - பாடடியவிக - கடருளாயபன்
ஒருல்லுலகின் - மீது - தொாருத   தி.

Ever worshipping and praising the flowery feet of Vámen, seated under his moon-like triple canopy, I will declare to the world, fully but concisely, oh damsel whose eyes are like sharp radiant spears, the poetic art.

தொருததுைாதத - மஙகளரு - சொல்லெழுததுத - தானம
வருததபா - இணடி - வருணம - பருததகா   ட
டபபாக - கதிகணமென் - நீைநதின் - றன்மையிண ச
செபபுவதா - முன்மொழியின்   சீர்.

It is a rule that in the first word the ten following characterislicks should be found united—good omen—precision of meaning—an unequal number of syllables—an initial of the proper order—of the proper gender —of the right nutritious quality—of the proper caste—of the right star —of the proper animal class—of the right order of feet.

சொருததுப - பொளுத - திருமணிநீர் - இஙகளெொ   ற்
காரபருழி - யாவண - கடருலகங - தோர்மவல   மன
கஙலக - நில்மபிநவுங - காணடகைய - பூனமொழிக   கு
மஙகலமாரு - சொலின்   வகை
வஙயுளி - சேர்தல் &c.

The following words and their synonymes are of good omen to appear as first words—சீர் - எழுததது - பொன - பூ - திரு - மணி நீர் இஙகள - சொல்-ளார் - பருழி - யாவண - கடல் - உலகம - தோர் - மவல் - மா - கவகை - நிலம - பிற ஞம.

The work consists of a hundred வெண்பா, which are all connected in this manner.

CHAPTER IV.

OF THE ART OF TAMIL POETRY.

SECTION THE FIRST.
OF POETICAL DICTION.

XCIX. The Tamils apply the general term இலக்கணம் to those works which contain the theory of any science, and இலக்கியம் to the models of their ancient writers in the several kinds of composition. Of the former, there is none which treats of the theory of poetry; my remarks, therefore, are deduced from its practice, as exhibited in the latter.

One branch of the art of poetry is the diction, for if this be not appropriate, we shall have mere metrical prose, not poetry. The Tamil poets, as I proceed to shew, use the genuine language of poetry; for,

C. First; they very rarely mention any object to which they do not couple some ornamental epithet: Thus, when they speak of a tree, they describe it either as green, or loaded with flowers, or shady, or majestically large, or as having all these qualities. Again, they never name a mountain, without representing it as rising among woods, or watered by fountains, or decked with flowers. Sometimes indeed, they employ this kind of embellishment to such an excess as to render the meaning obscure.

CI. Secondly. They are exceedingly fond of metaphorical expressions, such as உன்வயிறுாங்தவான், *a sword glutted with blood.* Thus, in Chintâmani, describing an amusement, where a number of chiefs are discharging their arrows at a wild boar brought from the mountains, the author says of a particular arrow.

புலியடபொாநியைமேைாநதுபுறங கொடுஃஉடடதனஐே.

மைஃமகளிலைமபஉம - அய்ஙு, கவி.

Scenting the thick bristles (as it glanced along them,) it pursued its flight.

If I should hereafter have sufficient leisure, it is my intention to make a collection of these expressions from their best authors, and thus to form a Tamil Parnassus: it will, therefore, be sufficient in this place, to apprize the reader, that the Tamil poets are extremely partial to figurative language; on which account, they very frequently employ a strain of uninterrupted allegory. In describing the life of a penitent, for instance, they compare it to a battle, or to the culture of land. The following example is taken from Chintâmaṅi. Speaking of charity, the author says,

உவாமுத - கிரவல்ர்க் - குடை மை - யுய்த்தவ   ॥

கவான - முத்ற - கூ.பபிய - க்கை - மாலை ழயா   ற்

நூஎஎஙிஷண - யடைகளா - தயஙகு - இநஙைஉஉஙீ   ॥

அவாடொவு௮ - முணடகட - லைஙைககபபடட   தே.

குணடஎஎவஸ்யாஙிலஸமடகம - கூ ம ஊ, ௪ஷி.

which may be thus rendered: *Virtue was the boundary to a raging sea of troubles, which was broken down by avarice: charity again repaired it with a mound of gold, heaped up by the hands of the poor.*

CII. Thirdly. The Tamils, then, make frequent use of allegories; and a poem in which this kind of ornament is used, is called சித்திரகஷி *a picture-like poem.* In their application of this figure, their extreme passion for hyperbole often leads them into extravagance. Thus, when they would extol a hero, they constantly compare his shoulders to a mountain. In the poem செகெந்தம, (*) the author, celebrating Tami-yēnti, the consort of his hero, says, that the god Brama, when about to create her form, (†) despising the elements of this world, took his materials from the concave surface of the moon; thereby leaving a scar, which is still apparent.

(*) The name of the poem is, properly, கைநடதம, which is the Sanskrit word கெநஷிம0, written according to Tamil orthography. This, being in the neuter gender, signifies *the poem in celebration of king* கெநஷிம8: the king's appellation கெநஷிம, is a derivative, formed according to the rules of Sanskrit grammar, from the name of his kingdom, கிஷிம். [See Wilkins' Sanskrit Grammar, Rule 882.

(†) The passage alluded to, speaks only of the face of Tamiyēnti. See அனைத கைததூஉ ஷிடடபடலம - மகூ, கஷி.

CIII. Fourthly. Like all the nations of the East, they delight in similies ; but those which they employ are, not unfrequently, strained, and such as the better judgment of Europeans would not approve. At the same time, they often make them a vehicle for moral instruction ; and this is esteemed a peculiar excellence. For instance, in Chintàmani, the author says of a crop of rice ;

செல்வமே-போற்றவஸ்-நிறுவித்-தேர்ஈததூாற்
கலவிசேர்-மாஈதநி-விஷறளுஷிக்-காய்த்த வே
நாடுஈசிறபபு-இமஈ,ஈவி.

The blade, when green, rears up its head, like a base man who possesses wealth ; but when it is ripe for the harvest, it is inclined, like the head of the wise. Again, Camben, in his Ràmàyanam, when relating how Ràmen slew a giantess named Tàdagei, says :

தொக்3ாலாஈருஈஈகடியவேஈச்ஈஉடுஈாஈஈகியஈேஈம   ஈ
ல்ஃஸ்ாஈஈஈுஈஈஈவடிஈவஈஈாஈஈஷேஈஈஸ்ஈஈ்றஈ ்
ஈஈ்டஈஈாஈஈஈநெஈஈ்றஈஈகாஈபஈஈஈஈஈ்றஈஈஈல்ஈா   ்
ஈஈ்ஈார்ஈஈஈல்ஈஈஈஈ்ஈஈஈஈஈஈஈஈஈஈஈயஈஈடபோஈஈறஈஈேற

இராமாயணம-முது:பால்காஈஈஈம-எ-வது-தாஈஈகஈஈதஈஈடஈம-
எஈஈ,ஈஈ.

Against the giantess, whose face wore the semblance of night, Rámen discharged an arrow, swift as speech, and flaming as fire ; which pierced her adamantine breast, and, indignant of delay, pursued its flight: so pass away the divine commands from the ears of the wicked. Similar instances are frequently to be met with.

CIV. Fifthly. In the Tamil poets we find many good instances of the figure hypotyposis, or vision, in which the subject is placed before the eyes in minute and faithful description.

The limits of my work do not admit of my adducing many instances. I shall only advert to one among several which occur in Chintàmani. The author places before your eyes a raging elephant which, impatient of control, carries death and destruction through the city, till he is caught and mounted by Sívagen himself, who, by his skilful management and by the awe which royalty inspires, subdues his fury, and, after guiding him whither he chooses, conducts him at last to the post, where he is bound and secured. The passage will be found towards the end of Canagamàleiár---llambacam.

SECTION THE SECOND.

OF POETIC FICTION.

CV. The Tamil poets indulge in the boldness of fiction, and employing their fancy on the actions of their deities, pay little regard to the laws of nature. The learned have been at much pains in defending Homer, who has, on one occasion, introduced a horse speaking: but the Tamil poets constantly attribute the power of speech to animals. In the poem Negizhdam, the principal agent is a swan, whom Naĺan, the hero of the story, employs as his ambassador. In their use of this license, however, they are so consistent, that a fiction employed in one place, is connected with those which follow; and they insert them so skilfully, that the vulgar look upon the dreams of the poets as real histories: and hence the numerous false notions which are prevalent in this country. Fiction appears to have some dependence on episode, which poets generally employ as a vehicle for their own conceits. Episodes are very frequently introduced by the Tamil poets, and with such art, that they seem not so much to be sought for, as to arise naturally out of the subject. Camben uses them to excess in his Ràmàyanam, where he relates no less than one thousand and eighty stories, which are almost all introduced by way of episode.

SECTION THE THIRD.

OF INVOCATION.

CVI. The Tamils maintain, that every kind of poem should commence with an invocation. They too, like us, have their Parnassus;

which, as I have already mentioned, is called Podiyamalei, and is a
mountain in the south of the peninsula, near Cape Comorin.   According to tradition, it was there the rules for the grammar and poetry of
this dialect were first invented, by a devotee named Agattiyan.(*)   It is
remarkable that they have neither an Apollo nor muses.   Their goddess
of science, or, if I may so term her, their Minerva, is called Saraswati.
To her, poets are supposed to be indebted for their skill and inspiration ;
on which account, she has received the following titles : கவிமகள், சொ
ற்கிழத்தி, பனுவலாட்டி, ஞானமூர்த்தி, நாமகள், இசைமடநதை, வாக்காள,
&c.   She is frequently invoked by poets in the commencement of their
works: thus, தணடியலங்காரம begins ;

சொல்லின்இழத்திமெல்லியவிணய   டி
சிந்தையைத்தியமபுவல்செயயுடகணிடெய &c.

*Meditating on thy delicate feet, oh thou sovereign lady of eloquence,
I will treat of the ornaments of poesy.*

It is more usual, however, to invoke some other of their divinities.
That every poem should commence with an invocation, is an established
rule, from which no deviation is allowed.

CVII.   On the subject of invocation, the precepts which have been
laid down, are numerous (†) and absurd.

(*) Agastya. SANSC.

(†)   The rules on this head are ten, called the தசப்பொருததம, of which Beschi
has only mentioned four, although it is evident that he was well acquainted with the
rest, because in No. XCIX, he quotes the stanzas of Venbàpàttiyel; in which the whole
are enumerated.   It may be worth while to supply what the author has omitted on this
curious, though unimportant, subject.   The ten rules are :

1st. மங்கலப்பொருததம. See No. CVII. Rule the first.

2d. சொற்பொருததம, an uncommon word, one having many meanings, or one
obscured by a violent change of letters, is not to be used as the commencing word.

3d. எழுத்துப்பொருததம. The commencing word must consist of three, five,
seven, or nine letters; but not of one, two, four, six or eight : a vowel, a consonant joined
with a vowel, and a mute consonant, are each reckoned as one letter.

4th. தானைபொருததம. There are five தானம், பாலதானம, குமரதானம,

There are three treatises, the work of different authors, which are exactly similar both in title and subject, being named பாட்டியல், that is, *the essence of poetry*. They differ only in the kind of verse in which they are respectively composed, one of them being written in வெண்பா, another in கலித்துறை, and the third in விருத்தம். They treat almost exclusively of invocation; respecting which, they lay down the following rules:

First. Some word must be selected, by which the poem and invocation are to commence, and the following twenty-three are assigned for this

இராசதானம், மூபபுததானம், மாணதானம்: to each of these, certain vowels are assigned, viz. அ, ஆ to பாலதானம்; இ, ஈ, ஊ, to குமரதானம்; உ, ஊ, ஔ, to இராசதானம்; எ, ஏ, to மூபபுததானம்; ஒ, ஓ, to மாணதானம். The first vowel, (whether joined with a consonant or not,) both of the hero's name, and of the commencing word of the poem, must belong to one of the first three தானம்.

5th. பாற்பொருத்தம். Gender is attributed to the letters: all the short letters are male; and all the long, female. There is, however, another mode of classing them, by which the twelve vowels are considered male; consonants joined with vowels, female; and mute consonants and ஆயதம், neuter. If the leading character of the poem be a male, the first letter of the invocation should be among the male class; if a female, of the female class. The neuter letters, according to the second mode, must never be used in the initial syllable. Little stress is laid upon the observance of this rule.

6th. உண்டி. The four vowels அ, இ, உ, எ, and the seven consonants க, ச, த, ந, ப, ம, வ, are called அமுதெதழுத்து, and are to be used in the first syllable: யா, யோ, ரா, ரோ, லா, லோ, வா, வோ, the consonants ய, ர, ல, வ, occurring in those combinations, the உயிரெனபெடை, and the ஒற்றெனபெடை, மகாக்குறுககம and ஆயதக்குறுககம are called நருடெசழுத்து, and are not to be used in the first syllable.

7th. வருணபபொருத்தம். See the text, No. CX.

8th. நாட்பொருத்தம். See the text, No. CVIII.

9th. கதிப்பொருத்தம். The nine letters அ, இ, உ, எ, க, ச, ட, த, ப, which are called தேவங்கி; and ஆ, ஈ, உள, எ, ஏ, ஞ, ண, ந, ம, which are called மக்கட்கி, are to be used in the initial syllable; ஓ, ஓ, ய, ர, ல, ழ, ற which are called விலங்கினகி; and ஈ, ஔ, வ, ள, ண, which are called நரங்கி, are not to be used in the initial syllable.

10th. கண்ப்பொருத்தம். See the text, No. CXI.

purpose: திரு, மணி, பூ, இலங்கா, ஞானம, சொல, சீர், எழுத்து, பொன,
தேர், புனல், கார், புயல், நிலம, கனகக, மஹி, உலகம, பரி, கடல், யாணை,
பருதி, அமுதம், புகழ். Every poem ought to begin with some one of
these words, or its synonyme. Accordingly, Iràmàyanam begins with
உலகம, Tandiyalangàram with சொல, and Venbàpàttiyel with மதி,
which is the same as இலங்கா. I have observed, however, that some
authors of the first repute have not conformed to this rule. The poem
Chintàmani begins with the word முடிவர், which the commentator explains
by முடியாத, and Pavananti commences his Nannùl with மலர்தலையுல
இன், where மலர் is not used in the sense of பூ, but is a participle from the
verb மலர்தல்; so that the commentator explains the word to mean,
the extended surface of the earth &c. In like manner, Silappadigàram
begins with the word குணவாயில், which answers to இழகது. The same
observation applies to many of the best Tamil poets.

CVIII. Secondly. The Tamil poets pay a superstitious regard to
the twenty-seven constellations. These, in order, are:

அசசுவினி	மகம	மூலம
பரணி	பூரம	பூராடம
கார்த்திகை	உதிரம	உததிராடம
உரோகணி	அததம	திருவோாணம
மிருகசீரிடம	இததினா	அவிட்டம
திருவாதினா	சுவாதி	சதயம
புனர்பூசம	விசாகம	பூராட்டாதி
பூசம	அனுடம	உததிராட்டாதி
ஆயிலியம	கேடடை	இரோவதி

To each of these they allot several letters, in the following manner:

அ - ஆ - இ - ஈ - கார்த்திகை	கொ - கோ - கௌ - பூசம	ஞா - ஜெரு - ஜெரா - அவி
உ - ஊ - எ - ஏ - ஐ - பூராடம		டடம
ஒ - ஓ - ஒள - உததிராடம	ச - சா - சி - சீ - - இரோவதி	த - தா - - - - - - சுவாதி
க - கா - கி - கீ - திருவோாணம	சு - சூ - செ - சே - சை - அசு	இ - ஜி - ஜு - ஜூ - தெ - தே
கு - கூ - - - - திருவாதினா	சுவிலி	தை - விசாகம
கெ - கே - கை - புனர்பூசம	சொ - சோ - சௌ - பரணி	தொ - தோ - தெள - சத
		யம

CIX. This being premised, look for the constellation which answers to the first letter in the name of your hero, and for that which answers to the first letter in the word with which your invocation begins : then reckon from one to the other, both inclusive, the number of constellations, according to the order in which we first enumerated them, observing, however, that, after you have counted the first nine, if there be so many, you must not go on to the tenth, but begin again with unity. So, likewise, if you should arrive at a second nine. If the number thus obtained, be one, three, five, or seven, the two constellations are said *not to accord with each other;* but if the number be two, four, six, eight, or nine, they do accord. Thus, the hero of the Iràmàyanam of Camben is named Iràmen, and the invocation commences with the word உலகம். Now, the constellation answering to the letter இ is கார்த்திகை, and that which answers to உ is பூராடம். Reckoning from கார்த்திகை to பூராடம், and leaving the first nine out of the account, the number which remains is nine; consequently, according to the foregoing rule, the two constellations in this case accord. This accordance is termed நட்பெருத்தம், or நட்சத்திரப்பொருத்தம்.

The preceding rule, it will be observed, is sufficiently absurd ; and is probably founded in superstition.

CX. Thirdly. The Tamils attribute the invention of the several letters of their alphabet to the following deities : the twelve vowels to Brúma ; அ, ஏ, to Siven ; ச, ஞ, to Vishnu ; ட, ண, to Subbramanien ; த, ந, to Dévéndren ; ப, ம, to Súrien ; ய, ர, to Chandren ; (for they consider the sun and moon to be deities, and worship them as such,) ல, வ, to Yamen, the god of death ; ழ, ள, to Varunen, Neptune ; ற, ன,

to Cupéren, Plutus. This being explained, our authors proceed to state what letters are applicable to each caste. To the Brahmans they assign the letters furnished by பிரமா, சிவன், விஷ்ணு, and சுபிரமணியன் ; namely, the twelve vowels, and க, ங, ச, ஞ, ட, ண : to kings, the letters furnished by தேதேவந்தொன, the sun, and moon ; namely, த, ந, ப, ம, ய, ர : to the mercantile caste, the letters furnished by the god of death, and Plutus ; namely, ல, வ, ழ, ன : to the வேளாளர் : the letters furnished by Neptune ; namely, ழு, ள : to the other castes, all the letters are common, except the vowels. On this head, the preceding remarks, with other information of still less importance, may be seen in the works named Pàttiyel, which I have already mentioned. A brief notice of them appears to me quite sufficient in this place.

CXI. Fourthly. They next lay down rules regarding the foot with which the invocation should begin. To this purpose they allot eight கணம், of which four are considered good, and four evil; obviously from superstitious motives. Those which are considered good, are :

First ; a foot consisting of three நேர், that is, a தேமாங்காய் ; which is termed இந்திரகணம், and augurs exaltation to the hero of the poem.

Second ; a foot consisting of a நிரை and two நேர், that is, புளிமாங்காய ; which is termed சந்திரகணம், and augurs everlasting life.

Third ; a foot consisting of three நிரா, that is, கருவிளங்கனி ; which is termed திலக்கணம், and augurs all kinds of happiness.

Fourth ; a foot consisting of நேர் and two நிரா, that is, கூவிளங்கனி which is termed நீர்க்கணம், and augurs a continuance of happiness. These four are called நற்கணம்.

The four which are considered evil, are called தீதகணம், and are as follows :

First ; a foot consisting of two நிரை and a நேர், that is, கருவிளங்காய ; which is termed அந்தகணம், and implies that the days of the hero's life shall be shortened.

Second; a foot consisting of two Gɛɾ and a நிஸா, that is இதுமாஎகணீ; which is termed வாயுகஎாை, and implies loss of wealth.

Third; a foot consisting of a நிஸா, a Gɛɾ, and a நிஸா; that is, புளிமா ங்கணி: which is termed நீக்கஎாை, and portends diseases.

Fourth; a foot consisting of a Gɛɾ, a நிஸா, and a Gɛɾ; that is, a கூடவி ஸாஉகாய: which is termed ருியஎஎாை, and portends that the hero's fortitude will forsake him. It is needless to remark, that all these rules have their origin in the grossest superstition.

SECTION THE FOURTH.

OF THE DIFFERENT KINDS OF POETRY.

CXII. 1st. Purànam. The word புராஎாை properly signifies *anti-quity*, but is here used in the sense of *history*. Those works, however, which the Tamils term புராஎாை, have neither the form, nor the truth, of history. They abound in fables, and are composed in poetry; being written in the kind of verse called விருத்தம. They differ from the epic poem, because they do not so readily admit of the introduction of episode, description, and other ornaments employed in that kind of composition.

CXIII. 2d. Epic poems, which they distinguish by the name of Càviyam, Càppiyam, and also Seyyul. In these compositions, they do not follow the rules prescribed by the Latin critics: they generally take up the narrative, or fable *ab ovo*, at the beginning. It is also an invariable rule, after the invocation, and the statement of the subject, to open the poem with a description of the hero's country, and of the capital where he is supposed to have reigned or flourished; and these are represented in the most favourable colours; not such as they are believed to have been, but such as the poet chooses to describe them. In this description, the rains which descend in the mountains, the streams which flow from them, and the consequent fertility of the country, never fail to have their place. These poems are divided into chapters, which are termed Saruccum, but more frequently Padalam, and occasionally Ilambacam. This last term is used when each chapter is appropriated to the relation of one complete event, such as a marriage or a victory. The poem Chintàmani is divided into chapters of this kind. If the poem is of considerable length, the whole is divided into books, which they term Càndam; and each book is subdivided, as before, into chapters. The Ràmayanam is divided into seven Càndams, or books ; and contains 128 Padalams, or chapters.

CXIV. 3d. They have a kind of elegy, which they denominate Ulá, or Málei, consisting of குறள்வெண்பா, which, as we explained in No. LXIX, may be rendered *distich*. I have there stated, that when a குறள் stands alone, it must always end with a foot of the first class ; that is, with a நாள், a மலர், a காசு, or a பிறப்பு: but since, in the species of poem which we are now describing, many குறள், or distichs, are joined together, this kind of foot is only used at the close of the elegy ; all the other distichs ending, not with a final foot, but with one belonging to either of the two classes இயற்சீர், or வெணசீர். Moreover, the several குறள் are linked together by the foot termed தனிசேசொல், which must come under the எதுகை of the குறள் which immediately precedes it.

The elegy, then, is constructed in the following manner: a line of four feet, one of three feet, then a தனிசேசொல்; the three under one எதுகை: a line of four feet, one of three, then a தனிசேசொல்: the three under one எதுகை, as before: and so on, to the last குறள், which must contain one line of four feet, and one of three; the third foot in the last being either a நாள், a மலர், a காசு, or a பிறப்பு. In this kind of poem, the rules which have been for the Venbá must be strictly observed ; and although all the feet of the இயற்சீர் class may be employed, yet, those called கருவிளம and கூவிளம are rarely used. The usual number of distichs, or Cúraí, is either 70, or 100, or 200. I shall give, as an example, a version or brief paraphrase, of the first psalm of David.

தீயோ - ருணைடிகளான - நீயோர் - வநிசடிசல்லா   ௱

நீயோர் - முறையோதான - டிசல்டிவாதன - தாயமறைச

சொலடிவலானடிற - டிதடகததான - டிசாரச - திராபபக   ற்

டிசல்டிவலானடிற - ரூமுணர்வான - டிசலடிவாடேன - டியாலடிஸ்னபயச   ய

நீர்முகததுப - டிபாயயா - நிறைநகனிடிகாய் - டிதாமடிபாபபச   ௬

கார்முகததுப - பாசிவிக்யுக - காய்நதுதிரா - - - - - - - - - - - - - சீர்முகததூ

மாகிலடேலார்க - டிகலலா - மயககஉற - வாழ்வா   டேம

யாசஎனோர்க - கபபடிடியோ - வனறஎடிற - - - - - - - - - - - டியசுடிபறக

காமமுதற - பறஉறுதலாற் - கால்சுஉறறுநக - தாடிஇய   ௫

ஈாமமுத - ல்ற்றறிவிார் - நசசநிவார் - - - - - - - - - - - - - - - வீமமிகத

தீர்வையிடு - நாளிற - இதைநடேதகஇ - நலலவரு   ட்

டிசார்வையுறத - தாமமிநிகது - ரூழநதுவிஸ்வார் - - - - - - - - - டிபார்வையில்

தூயோர் - டிநநியநிவான - ரூழான்வான - டிகஇ௫௬௬   ௬

நீயோர் டிநநிய நிவான - டிசார்நது

Observe, that, although the தஇசடிசால் here comes under the எதுக of the preceding குறள், it is connected, in signification, with the குறள் which follows.

CXV. 4th. Parani. A kind of poem, which, like the last, consists of a succession of couplets, but differs from it, in wanting the intermediate தஇசடிசால், and in having its lines of equal length. The lines are constructed according to the rules for the விருததம, and consequently, neither the connexion of the feet, nor their number, is fixed, and frequent use is made of the குறிபபு.

The remarks on the விருததம are equally applicable to this kind of poem; the only difference being that, in the விருததம, each stanza must consist of four lines, and in this, of two.

CXVI. 5th. Calambacam. A sort of poetry, in which the author mixes at pleasure all these kinds of verse: அகவல, டிவணபா, கஇபபச, வருஇபபா, மருட்பா, தாழிசை, துறை, விருததம. This variation in the measure, renders the composition pleasing to the ear, but difficult to those who compose or recite it.

CXVII. 6th. Ammànei. This kind of poem is so little esteemed, that those who value themselves on their poetical character, universally despise it; the consequence of which is, that no example of it is to be found in any ancient author of repute. It consists of couplets, the component lines of each coming under one உதை, and being of the kind termed அளவடி, that is, lines of four feet. These feet may be of the classes வெண்சீர் and இயற்சீர், but the two species கருவிளம், and கூவிளம், are hardly ever used. With regard to the connexion of the feet, it is considered best to conform to வெண்டளை : this rule, however, is not so absolute but that it admits of occasional deviation. The natives do not compose these verses on any settled principle, but only by ear. In order to relieve the wearisomeness of a monotonous cadence, they often introduce two or three intermediate lines, of the measure விருத்தம், in which they state briefly the subject on which they are about to enlarge. The diction ought to be perfectly familiar; and, on this account, it is usual to abstain from the bolder and more poetical tropes and figures, the use of which is so frequent in other kinds of poetry. Accordingly, fiction and episode are considered inadmissible. This kind of poem is employed in recounting the histories or lives of their deities, princes, &c.; and, like the epic poem, commences with an invocation, and then enters at large upon the praises of the country and city of the hero.

CXVIII. 7th. Of the remaining kinds of poetry, there are two called Vannàm and Sindu, which are in very frequent use. The வண்ணம consists of eight equal stanzas, each of which is termed கவி : as, முதற் கவி, இரண்டாஙகவி, &c.

The first stanza contains an invocation of some deity, and his praises; the second describes the kingdom of the person whom it is intended to celebrate; the third and fourth contain his name and praises; and the four remaining stanzas treat of his women, and here they generally introduce observations highly offensive to delicacy.

All the stanzas should be equal, and they are constructed with reference, not to metre, but to harmony, the degree of which depends on the pleasure of the poet. The harmony should occur three times in every கலி. Each stanza closes with a deep tone, which they term தாகல; and so on, through the eight கலி. The எதுகை, however, is not repeated eight times, but only four; namely, in the first, the third, the fifth, and the seventh கலி. The other கலி must have the consonance called மோனை; that is, each must begin with the same letter as the one which immediately precedes it.

CXIX. 8th. Sindu. This contains four stanzas, the first of which is preceded by a short intercalary line, called பல்லவம், which is repeated before each of the others. Of the four stanzas, the first is shorter than the rest, and is distinguished by the name அதுபல்லவம. The other three are similar to each other in every respect; and, like those mentioned in the last number, are not formed by any rule, but with such degree of harmony as the writer pleases. In this kind of poem, besides the எதுகை, it is common to use the இயைபு; which, as has been explained in No. LXVI, is that consonance of verses which depends on similarity in their termination. The சிந்து is reckoned so low an order of poetry, that the learned think it beneath them to recite it.

CXX. Dramatic poetry is so completely disregarded, that the ancient writers have left us neither models of it, nor rules for its composition: the natives are, nevertheless, extremely fond of dramatic representations. Short comedies are termed கூத்து, while tragedies and tragi-comedies are called நாடகம், and, on the sea coast, வாசகப்பா. These are all written in various kinds of verse; among which, the சிந்து is constantly introduced. In representation, they are always accompanied with singing and dancing; but they display no higher degree of skill or contrivance than is sufficient to please the vulgar and to excite mirth: to search for any art in them, would, therefore, be a useless attempt.

In conclusion, I have to observe, that, in speaking of the superior dialect, or செந்தமிழ், authors subdivide it into three kinds, comprised in the term முத்தமிழ், that is, *the three sorts of Tamil.* Each kind has its separate name: the first is called இயற்றமிழ், or *prose Tamil;* the second, இசைத்தமிழ், or *poetical Tamil;* the third, நாடகத்தமிழ் or *the Tamil of the drama.* This remark will suffice to show, how far they are correct, who maintain, that the higher dialect ought to be termed the *poetical* dialect.

For EU product safety concerns, contact us at Calle de José Abascal, 56–1°,
28003 Madrid, Spain or eugpsr@cambridge.org.

www.ingramcontent.com/pod-product-compliance
Ingram Content Group UK Ltd.
Pitfield, Milton Keynes, MK11 3LW, UK
UKHW030856150625
459647UK00021B/2791